QUEBEC

Text by

BRUNO BLOCISZEWSKI

Crescent Books
New York

Translation:
Alison L'Eplattenier

End papers: View in winter of a little old town of the "Chemin du Roy", along the St. Lawrence near Quebec. Title page: The famous Château Frontenac, at Quebec.

Designed and produced by
Editions Minerva SA

First English edition published by
Editions Minerva SA

Copyright © 1984 by
Minerva Editions S.A., Genève.

This 1984 edition is published
by Crescent Books.
Distributed by Crown Publishers, Inc.

Printed in Italy

Library of Congress Cataloging
in Publication Data

ISBN: 0-517-439433

QUEBEC

Quebec is one of the ten provinces of Canada but its population of more than six millions inhabitants represents about a quarter of the total population of the country.

Of these 6,300,000 Quebecers, 80% speak French, 10% speak English and 10% belong to different ethnic communities. Quebec is the only province in Canada of which the majority of the population is French-speaking.

It is a huge territory, 601,170 sq. miles, as large as the two Germanies, Spain, Portugal, France, Belgium and Switzerland put together! The population is almost entirely concentrated in the plain of the St. Lawrence, to the south of Quebec, and especially in the two large cities of the province: Montreal, the great metropolis, and Quebec, the capital.

Water is everywhere in Quebec. The St. Lawrence, one of the largest rivers in the world, crosses the south of the province over a distance of 2,300 miles. As for lakes, there are about 400,000 of them! The forest (covering 449,218 sq. miles) also represents one of the most important elements in the landscape of the province.

Subject to the influence of continental masses and Arctic sea currents, this vast region is known to have a very harsh climate. The snowy season lasts about 12 or 13 weeks in the area around Montreal and can reach as much as 23 weeks in the Côte-Nord region of the St. Lawrence. In January and February the average temperature falls well below zero. In summer, on the other hand, it is very hot and humid. As for the spring and autumn, they are both superb, with nature bursting out in spring after the long winter, and the forests taking on fantastic shades of colour in the autumn.

The history of this territory began in 1534, when Jacques Cartier took possession of Canada in the name of the king of France, but the French only came back into this region at the beginning of the 17th century. Samuel de Champlain founded the city of Quebec in 1608 and Paul de Chomedey from Maisonneuve founded Montreal in 1642. There followed many bitter conflicts with the Iroquois.

While thousands of English immigrants settled in New England there were still only 2,500 French settlers in New France in 1663. New France was difficult to organize from an administrative point of view, because of the long distance from the metropolis and also because of its status as a colony. One century later there were a million and a half English people and still only 80,000 French.

The English and the French fought against each other, however, both in North America and in Europe. But in 1759, the English troops won the battle of the Heights of Abraham at Quebec and in 1760, Montreal in its turn fell into the hands of the English. Then, through the Treaty of Paris (1763), France handed over New France to Great Britain. The English regime followed on from the French regime.

The year 1791 saw the division of Canadian territory into two provinces: Lower Canada (of which the capital was Quebec), mainly French-speaking, and Upper Canada (capital Toronto), mainly English-speaking. Feeling that they lacked the most elementary of rights and powers, the French Canadians tried to organize a revolt. This was the Rebellion of the Patriots (1837-38), led by Louis-Joseph Papineau.

The Act of British North America, of 1867, created the Canadian Confederation, reuniting the provinces of New Scotland, New Brunswick, Ontario and Quebec. Quebec society was at that time essentially rural, directed by the clergy, industry being in the hands of English Canadians.

Successive governments of the province were, moreover, to have a tendency to leave the control of the economy to the English Canadians as well as to American companies. But, in 1960, the Liberal Party of Jean Lesage came into power: this was the "Quiet Revolution" which was beginning, a period of awakening on the part of the Quebecers and a taking in hand of the economy.

General de Gaulle in 1967 proclaimed his famous "Vive le Québec libre" (Long live Free Quebec!) from the balcony of the City Hall in Montreal, and the following year, the Quebec Party was created canvassing in favour of independence. Headed by René Levesque, it came to power in 1976 but in 1980, a referendum proposing the independence of the province resulted in 59% of the voters rejecting the proposal.

Today, the economy depends mainly on hydro-electric power, (it is one of the regions of the world which is best supplied with hydro-electric resources), mines, forests and agriculture. For some years, Quebec has been attempting the revalorization of its natural wealth.

When one visits Quebec for the first time, one is struck by the personality of its inhabitants. They are, as it were, an amalgam of the various cultures inherited from the French and the English, the Americans and even the Amerindians. From these different contributions, a modern Quebec has emerged, and an original, pleasant society, that is known, especially in France, through its talented singers, but whose dynamism has spread to all sectors of life, both cultural and social.

Three views of Quebec showing its variety. Montreal, the very large North American metropolis; in wild countryside, a trapper in his canoe, similar to so many others which have become legendary in the country, and the beautiful coast of Gaspé, which has remained unchanged for centuries.

THE CHARMS OF MONTREAL

The metropolitan area of Montreal has a population of about three million, the town of Montreal itself over a million.

But when Jacques Cartier arrived in 1535 within sight of the island from which rose the mountain that he himself called "Mont-Royal", it was an Indian settlement, Hochelaga, which occupied the site of the future metropolis. About 3,500 Indians lived there. Then when Samuel de Champlain stopped at the same spot seventy-five years later, the village no longer existed. It had probably disappeared as the result of a tribal war.

It was in 1608 that Champlain founded Quebec, but it was not until 17th May 1642 that Paul de Chomedey, Master of Maisonneuve, founded Ville-Marie, which was later to become Montreal. About forty settlers had followed him, in the hope of evangelizing the Indians.

Conflicts with the Iriquois Indians began almost at once and continued until 1701, at which time the town had a population of 2,000 inhabitants. There were 5,000 in 1763, almost all of French origin.

For the whole of the 18th century the fur trade represented the most important source of revenue for Montreal.

Now 65% of Montrealers speak French, so that Montreal is the second largest French-speaking city in the world, after Paris. Just over 20% of the inhabitants have English as their mother-tongue, and large ethnic communities— Italians, Chinese, Jews, Greeks, amongst others— give Montreal its cosmopolitan character.

The *Rue Saint-Laurent,* perpendicular to the river, separates the town into two sections, east and west. The eastern part is mainly French-speaking, the west English-speaking, although this old linguistic separation is gradually weakening year by year, with many French-speakers coming to settle in the western suburbs.

The visitor is often struck at first by how American-looking Montreal is, with the un-avoidable, ever-present skyscrapers in the centre of the town. The discovery of Old Montreal or the streets where people carry on their conversations sitting on the steps outside their houses will give a different idea of the town. A walk through the areas where restaurants and cafés abound will give a foretaste of its very special atmosphere. The charm of Montreal does not have an immediate effect on the first day, but after one has succumbed to it, one cannot easily live without it.

OLD MONTREAL (AROUND THE PLACE JACQUES-CARTIER)

The *Place Jacques-Cartier* is the centre of the lively activity of Old Montreal. Cafés, restaurants and bars with music are parti-cularly numerous here, as well as in the nearby streets. It is in this part of the town too that craftsmen and portrait-sketchers carry on their trade.

In the *Rue Notre-Dame,* north of the *Place Jacques-Cartier,* stands the City Hall. Inaugurated in 1878, it was almost entirely destroyed by fire in 1922, which left only the outside walls standing. Also in the *Rue Notre-Dame* is the Silver Dollar Saloon, so called because the owner has inlaid 350 silver dollars in the floor. The customers can thus boast of having walked over a small fortune ! Ramezey Castle faces the City Hall across the street. Claude de Ramezay was governor of Montreal from 1703 to 1724, and the castle which bears his name, built in 1705, now houses one of the most interesting historical museums in the town. On the death of Claude de Ramezay in 1755, the castle was sold to the East India Company, and was used in 1775 as the headquarters of the American army of occupation, under General Richard Montgomery and General Benedict Arnold. Benjamin Franklin once stayed there.

South of the *Place Jacques-Cartier,* the *Rue Saint-Paul* is known for its bars and their music, which even spreads out into the street.

The fine Bonsecours Market, with its cupola and its columns, was built between 1845 and 1852. In 1849 it was, for a few days, the seat of the Parliament of United Canada. Then it became the City Hall from 1852 to 1878, and finally a public market until 1964.

Not far from there are to be found two buildings worthy of interest; the Calvet House (1725), typical of the architecture of the 18th cen-tury in Quebec, and Papineau House, which was

Montreal. Above and opposite: The City Hall and the Place Jacques-Cartier. *Right: Buildings in the traditional French style of olden days, the noble "Marché Bon Secours" and the nearby church, Notre-Dame-de-Bonsecours — the oldest in Montreal.*

the residence of Louis-Joseph Papineau, a French-Canadian statesman, one of the leaders of the rebellion of the French-Canadians against the English-Canadians in 1837.

The Notre-Dame Chapel of Bonsecours is the oldest church in Montreal. Begun in 1657 on the initiative of Marguerite Bourgeoys, the founder of the Notre-Dame Congregation, the chapel had to be rebuilt in 1771 after a disastrous fire. As it is a tradition for sailors to gather there when they have narrowly missed being shipwrecked, the chapel has become known as "the sailors' church". A statue of the Virgin Mary stands high above it, facing the harbour. There is a museum there which relates episodes in the life of Marguerite Bourgeoys, using hand-made dolls. Miniature boats have also been left by sailors as votive offerings. Visitors can climb right to the top of the chapel, from where one has a magnificent view from a belvedere over the St. Lawrence River, the harbour, the island of Sainte-Hélène and the island of Notre-Dame.

OLD MONTREAL (THE PLACE D'ARMES, CHURCH OF NOTRE-DAME)

In the centre of the *Place d'Armes* stands the statue of Paul de Chomeday, Master of Maisonneuve, founder of Montreal in 1642. This sculpture, the work of Philippe Hébert, represents Maisonneuve holding the banner of France. He is surrounded by Louis Hébert, the first Canadian settler, Jeanne Mance, the founder of the *Hôtel-Dieu*, an Iroquois, and Lambert Closse, one of Maisonneuve's lieutenants, who was in charge of defending the fort for four years and who is represented with his dog Pilot, renowned for sniffing out the Iroquois enemy. The famous words of

Maisonneuve engraved on the monument read: "It is an honour to accomplish my mission, even if all the trees on the island of Montreal were to change into as many Iroquois."

The Church of Notre-Dame is one of the most remarkable in North America. It is in neo-Gothic style, was erected between 1824 and 1829, and is the work of the Irish architect James O'Donnell, who was a Protestant but was converted to Catholicism during the building of the church!

The twin towers, names Temperance and Perseverance, stand 230 feet high. They were added in 1841 and 1842. In the West Tower, a bell called John the Baptist, or The Great Bell, weighs

as much as 11,260 kilogrammes! It used to need a dozen men to ring it; today it works by electricity but is only used on important occasions.

The church can seat 5,000 people, the interior being designed by the French-Canadian architect Victor Bourgeau. The monumental altar and the huge throne are particularly impressive and the organ, one of the most powerful in America, boasts 5,772 pipes. The eleven stained-glass windows, which relate the religious history of the town and the most important stages in its founding and development, were installed in the church in 1929.

To the right of the Church of Notre-Dame stands the Old Seminary of Saint Sulpice, the most

ancient building in Montreal (dating back to 1685), erected by the Sulpicians, who arrived in Ville-Marie in 1657. The wooden clock was added later, in 1710, and is thought to be the oldest of its kind in the whole of America. This too works by electricity now.

If one takes the *Rue Saint-Sulpice*, which goes off to the left of the church of Notre-Dame, then the *Rue Saint-Paul*, one finally reaches the *Place Royale*, the oldest square in the town. It is at this spot that, on the 16th March 1644, Maisonneuve drove back an attack by the Iroquois, killing their chief himself. On an obelisk which has been erected in the *Place Royale* an inscription reads: "On the 18th May 1642, Paul Chomedey of Maisonneuve laid the foundations of the town of Montreal. On the 23rd February 1642, Montreal had been dedicated to the Virgin Mary under the name of Ville-Marie. The first settlers in Ville-Marie have their names inscribed on this obelisk. Next one should make one's way to the *Place d'Youville*. It is also worth going a little out of one's way to see the Youville stables, harmoniously grouped buildings of grey stone dating from the 19th century.'

Old Montreal. Left: A restaurant sign and the **Rue Saint-Paul.** *The* **Place d'Armes** *with the monument of Maisonneuve, founder of the town. This page: A view of the* **Place d'Youville** *and the richly-decorated interior of the Church of Notre-Dame.*

THE EASTERN SECTORS

The population of the eastern part of Montreal is overwhelmingly French-speaking. The different areas of this part of the town are, generally speaking, much less luxurious than those of the west.

The night life, for the French-speakers of Montreal, is very concentrated around the *Rue Saint-Denis* and the streets perpendicular to it. This whole area is called the "Latin Quarter" a name given to it after the opening of the numerous schools of higher education, as well as the University of Montreal, about the beginning of this century. At that time, the Latin Quarter was the centre of an active cultural life. The removal of the University of Montreal to another part of the town in 1943, left this Latin Quarter with serious economic problems, which also brought an end to its lively activities. From the middle of the 60's onwards, however, the streets of this area have been livened up again by the opening up of a large number of restaurants, cafés and shops in the *Rue Saint-Denis,* especially between the *Rue Sainte-Catherine* and the *Rue Sherbrooke.*

In the square formed by the streets of Sainte-Catherine, Berri, Saint-Denis and the Maisonneuve Boulevard, another university, the University of Quebec at Montreal, was established in 1979.

Saint-Louis Square, further north, is a spot much sought after by artists. The curious Victorian-type houses which surround this garden form a most original group of buildings architecturally.

The little *Rue Prince-Arthur,* which can ben reached from the Place Saint-Louis, has become another lively centre of activity in the eastern part of the town.

Countless restaurants have crowded into the small area reserved for the pedestrian zone.

A little further north, one enters the Mont-Royal Plateau, a working-class district, with the typical streets of this kind of area, lined with houses, whose upper floors are reached by outside staircases, on which in fine weather, the Montrealers often gather to sit and discuss topics of all kinds until well into the night.

The *Avenue Duluth* has developed in much the same way as the *Rue Prince-Arthur.* The inevitable restaurants and especially, in the whole of the area, antique shops and craft shops can be found every few yards.

Lafontaine Park, covering an area of about 100 acres, is one of the most delightful parks in the town. The western section is laid out as an English Garden, with two artificial lakes, on which boats are for hire, and well-designed, well-tended lawns. The eastern part has been arranged as a French Garden, with straight paths marked out on a flat stretch of land. Inside the park, the visitor must not miss the "jardin des merveilles", a zoo for children, in which the animals move about in fairy-tale settings and the land of fables.

A little further east lies the Botanical Garden, a particularly pleasant spot. It is considered to be one of the most beautiful in the world of its kind. It was founded in 1931 by the Friar Marie-Victorin, a famous naturalist from Quebec, and it can now boast a collection of more than 20,000 species and varieties of plants, which are divided into some thirty different sections.

Montreal. Left: A view of the **Rue Saint-Denis** *and one of its numerous cafés; the vast Olympic Stadium, a snowy street and the sign of the* **Rue Prince-Arthur.** *Right and following pages: Houses typical of the Old Town.*

THE WESTERN SECTOR

The vast majority of the English-speakers in Montreal live in the area situated towards the west of the town, but more and more of the French-speakers have been coming to settle there over the past few years.

If one winds one way from the *Rue Université* up the *Rue Sainte-Catherine* towards the west, one passes, or stops to look at, the big stores, which are grouped together here over a distance of some hundred yards or so. One also passes the *Place Phillips,* a little haven of peace amongst all the bustling activity of the shops.

On the right-hand side of the street rises the Anglican Cathedral, Christ Church (built in 1859). This very elegant cathedral is a fine example of gothic architecture. Designed by an Englishman, Frank Wills, it was eventually completed by the Montreal architect, Thomas S. Scott. It was originally topped by a stone spire, but this had to be replaced in 1927 by an aluminium spire.

Turning left into the *Rue Peel,* one finds oneself in the *Place Dominion,* a vast open space, laid out as a garden, around which are grouped some remarkable buildings. A century ago, when Montreal had not yet become the great city it is today, a cemetery occupied all this sector. On the side opposite Dorchester Boulevard, the square continues into the *Place du Canada.* Around these two pleasantly green squares, three buildings especially attract the visitor's attention: the Cathedral of *Marie-Reine-du-Monde* (Mary Queen of the World), Windsor Station and the Anglican church, St. George's.

The Catholic Cathedral of *Marie-Reine-du-Monde* was built between 1870 and 1894, on a plan designed by the Montreal architect Victor Bourgeau, at the request of Mgr Bourget, the second Bishop of Montreal. It is a reproduction, half the original size, of the basilica of St. Peter's in Rome.

Windsor Station (1889) is the work of the American architect Bruce Price, who designed the famous Frontenac Castle at Quebec. Of special note in the station, which looks like a castle, is the superb glass roof in the

waiting-hall.

The *Place Dominion* and the *Place du Canada* are surrounded by skyscrapers, mostly occupied by hotels and offices. The *Place Bonaventure* and the *Place Ville-Marie,* the main centres of the underground town are only a short distance away.

The streets called, Stanley, Drummond, de la Montagne, Crescent and Bishop, which run at right angles to the *Rue Sainte-Catherine,* are for the western part of the town what the *Rue Saint-Denis* and the *Rue Prince-Arthur* are for the east: very busy and crowded by day and still full of life in the evening too.

At the same level, on Sherbrooke, stands the Fine Arts Museum. Founded in 1860, it is the oldest museum in Canada. The present building dates from 1912, and its neo-classical facade contrasts strangely with the modern interior, in which are displayed, not only a permanent collection, but also a number of temporary exhibitions. Close by, the Church of Saint Andrew and Saint Paul is considered to be one the finest churches in the town.

Montreal. The campus of McGill University, the elegant Rue Sherbrooke *and the picturesque* Rue Crescent. *Opposite and above: The chancel and a view from above of the Cathedral of Marie-Reine-du-Monde, a replica of the basilica of St. Peter in Rome. Right: the old city, taken from the wealthy quarter of Westmount.*

THE CITY CENTRE
THE UNDERGROUND TOWN

Although situated to the west of the *Rue Saint-Laurent* which divides the east from the west, the *Place des Arts* and the *Complexe Desjardins* could be said to be situated in fact in what is called the City Centre.

The *Place des Arts* is composed of two different buildings: the Wilfrid Pelletier Hall (built in 1963), a concert hall in which the Montreal Symphony Orchestra performs, and a second building, inaugurated in 1967, consisting of two theatres one above the other.

The *Complexe Desjardins,* on the other side of the *Rue Sainte-Catherine,* was designed and built through the common effort and collaboration of the Desjardins Cooperative Movement and the Government of the province of Quebec. Inaugurated in 1976, it consists of a vast central square, several floors on different levels *(les basilaires),* occupied by shops of all kinds, administrative buildings and a hotel.

The *Complexe Desjardins* is part of the famous "underground town" of Montreal, of which the *Place Ville-Marie* and the *Place Bonaventure* were the original foundations. This "underground town" allows Montrealers to have access to all the services and facilities of a normal town without their having to go out into the open air, and thus being protected from the bad weather.

These large commercial centres, consisting of hundreds of separate shops, are linked by the metro. It is not impossible to imagine the day when all these underground centres of activity might be linked together by means of corridors, and so giving pedestrians a chance to move about over the whole of the territory of Montreal, under cover.

The *Place Ville-Marie,* opened in 1962, has given new life to the city centre, with more than 20,000 people work there. The total length of all its corridors represents something like six miles. The *Place Bonaventure* is even more spectacular. It is used as a centre for exhibitions and shows of all kinds.

The Montreal metro was inaugurated in 1966, with 26 stations. It has gradually been added to in almost every direction, and when it is finally finished, in about 1990, there will be nearly a hundred different stations.

McGill University lies to the west of the *Place des Arts,* at the foot of Mont-Royal. This university, known the world over, occupies the site of the former property of James McGill, a politician and businessman who, in the year 1813, gave up the land and gave a large sum of money towards the creation of the university.

If one continues one's journey down the *Rue Université* one will arrive in the *Place Victoria,* after having crossed the *Rue Sainte-Catherine* and the Dorchester Boulevard. The *Place Victoria* building, about 550 feet high, immediately strikes the eye. Naturally enough, a statue of Queen Victoria (dating from 1872) stands in a prominent position, and the entrance to the metro is decorated by a gate dating from the end of the 19th century, offered by the city of Paris. This is an especially good viewpoint for looking out over the remarkable cluster of skyscrapers of the city centre.

Top: The **Place Ville-Marie** *and its skyscrapers. The "underground" town of Montreal allows its inhabitants to avoid going out into the harsh Canadian winter; the Desjardins Centre (left, and following pages,) the arcades in the* **Place Bonaventure** *(top right) and the stores in the* **Alexis Nihon Centre** *(opposite).*

A COSMOPOLITAN THOROUGHFARE

It is the *Rue Saint-Laurent,* which lies perpendicular to the river, that marks the dividing line between the eastern and western sectors of the town.

The *Rue Saint-Laurent,* often called simply "La Main" (from the English "Main Street"), is the street of the different ethnic communities. Jewish immigrants from Russia settled here towards the end of the 19th or at the beginning of the 20th century, to such an extent that at that time yiddish was the language the most widely spoken on this thoroughfare. A little later, at the beginning of this century, Greeks also came to find a home here, as did other immigrants of different nationalities: first Slavs, then Latin-Americans and Portuguese, so that the present *Rue Saint-Laurent* is the reflection of this succession of new arrivals, each community having opened up its own shops and its own restaurants, in which the different products typical of their countries of origin are to be found. Thus it is possible to discover over a distance of only a few hundred yards, the extremely cosmoplitan nature of this great metropolis.

The Chinese Quarter is situated in the area south of the *Rue Saint-Laurent,* in the *Rue de la Gauchetière* and the neighbouring streets. Considerably smaller than the Chinese Quarter of New York, the one in Montreal nevertheless has a

certain charm. One striking particularity is the way the telephone booths are decorated in Chinese style. The first Chinese immigrants came to Canada about 1860 in order to escape the famine in China. They found work mainly in the gold mines in British Columbia, but the very hard working conditions drove many of them to settle in the east of Canada, especially in Montreal and Toronto.

The number of Chinese who actually live in the Chinese Quarter is very small, but the area is nevertheless very lively, especially on Sundays, when the shops are not closed, and the Chinese colony in Montreal like to gather and talk. The best Chinese restaurants in the town are, of course, to be found in this area.

North of the *Rue Saint-Laurent,* near the metro stations of Beaubien and Jean-Talon, lies the Italian Quarter, with its shops selling salamis, wine, pasta and other Italian products. In the streets, the Quebec accent is mostly replaced by the rapid singing intonation of the Italian language.

Montreal. Above, left and right: two different views of the **Rue Sainte-Catherine,** *the most important thoroughfare in the town. Opposite: The Anglican Cathedral and one of the buildings in the* **Place des Arts.** *Right: The Eaton Centre and the neon signs at night in the "Broadway" of Montreal.*

MONT-ROYAL, OUTREMONT AND WESTMOUNT

Even in the very heart of the city, Mont-Royal stands out for everyone to see, dominating the town. It rises to a height of some 700 feet and gives Montreal a special charm of its own.

It was Jacques Cartier himself who, when he was invited by the Indians to climb it right to the top, is said to have given it its name, by crying out *"Quel mont royal!"* ("What a royal mountain!")

Mont-Royal park was planned and laid out in 1894 by the famous landscape-gardener Frederick Law Olmsted, who was also responsible for New York's Central Park, amongst others.

Winding paths run round the park, and an artificial lake, Beavers' Lake *(le lac des Castors)* attracts a number of interested visitors. The park is an ideal spot for those who want to stroll about at leisure, and welcomes hundreds of thousands of visitors each year, even in winter, as there are also facilities for, amongst other sports, skiing and skating. One should not leave the park without the traditional visit to the observation post, from where one can admire the fine view over the town.

Squirrels are the real inhabitants of Mont-Royal. They can be seen everywhere and are so tame that they come and eat out of the visitors' hands.

To the east of Mont-Royal, the *Avenue du Parc* is a cosmopolitan street. In the 40's and 50's, it was the heart of the Jewish Quarter of Montreal, but now has a large number of Greek restaurants.

The autonomous municipality of Outremont is rather for the French-speakers what Westmount represents for the English-speakers. Fine residences are to be found there, and many open spaces and grassy stretches, but there are

also, especially on the *Avenue Laurier* and *Avenue Bernard,* restaurants, cafés, book-shops and original boutiques which give Outremont a special atmosphere of its own, much appreciated by the Montrealers.

Situated to the west of Mont-Royal Park is the campus of the University of Montreal, the largest French-speaking university outside France.

At the end of the *Chemin de la Côte-des-Neiges,* which is a very busy street, one reaches St. Joseph's Oratory, one of the most important places of pilgrimage in America. The Oratory is the work of Friar André, a very simple, modest man, with a deep feeling of devotion for St. Joseph. He has been credited with countless examples of miraculous healing, and it was he who built a little wooden chapel on this site in 1904. The crypt was added in 1917 and the basilica, begun in 1924, was only completed in 1955. It is an impressive edifice, its dome, about 100 feet in diameter, being the largest in the world after that of St. Peter's in Rome.

At the end of last century, the autonomous municipality of Westmount numbered 95% English-speakers amongst the inhabitants. The percentage today is much lower, since the separation between the two linguistic communities is becoming less and less marked. Westmount is still considered, though as the most luxurious town in the province of Quebec. Sumptuous 19th-century residences are no rarity, and the *Avenue Green* and the *Avenue Rosemount* are part of an area in which it is most pleasant to stroll. Further north lies Summit Park, surrounded by huge houses, by which the tourists are always most impressed and amazed.

In winter and in summer, Mont-Royal Park offers its visitors a great many possibilities, with its winding paths which are ideal for walking, its squirrels, amusing to watch and very tame, its cross-country skiing tracks and its fine belvedere, from which one has a magnificent view over the town and the St. Lawrence.

THE ST. LAWRENCE AT MONTREAL, THE ISLANDS

The islands of *Sainte-Hélène* can be reached by crossing the huge Jacques-Cartier Bridge. Built in 1930, it is about two miles long and stands 150 feet high. The island was given its name by Samuel de Champlain in 1611, in honour of the woman who had been his wife for twelve years, Hélène Boulé.

The island has a surface of some 300 acres and was used as a fortress from 1822 to 1824. Its old fort now houses the Military and Maritime Museum, which traces the military history of New France from the beginning of the 15th century.

In summer, historical events are re-enacted with soldiers in period costume taking part: the Free Companies of the Marine, which were in 1683 the first permanent militia in Canada, and Fraser's Highlanders, a regiment which came to Canada in 1757, and which fought under the command of General Wolfe, victorious in the battle of the Plains of Abraham, at Quebec, Fifes, drums and bagpipes are much in evidence.

But the great attraction on the island of *Sainte-Hélène* is without any doubt *Terre des Hommes*, an exhibition which has taken advantage of the former premises and facilities of the Univer-sal Exhibition which was held in Montreal in 1967. Numerous pavilions and hundreds of shows of all kinds draw millions of visitors there every summer. One can quite easily spend a whole day at *Terre des Hommes* and thus take advantage of all the activities which are put on in the different pavi-

Montreal. Left: The skyscrapers and the metro together (the "Berri de Montigny" metro station). Above: Two canons from the old fort of the Island of Sainte-Hélène. Below: Jacques-Cartier Bridge and, on the banks of the St. Law-rence, the Tower of Victoria Quay.

lions, each with its own theme (Humour, Environment, etc.) and in those reserved for the countries which created them.

In addition to all this, one also finds on the island of *Sainte-Hélène*, not only the Montreal Aquarium, but a vast fair-ground, called *La Ronde* (the Roundabout), whose lights irresistibly attract one's attention when one crosses the Jacques-Cartier Bridge at night.

The island of *Notre-Dame* is a totally artificial island. It was the setting for the International Floral Festival in 1980, a festival which has been held here again each summer since then. One can stroll amidst the many flower-beds, each one designed by gardeners of a different nationality.

Not far from here is the *Cité du Havre*, where one must visit the Museum of Contemporary Art, founded in 1964. One cannot help being struck by a futuristic complex of modular apartments, designed by the architect Moishe Safdie, and called "Habitat 67".

Montreal Harbour is the largest on the east coast of Canada, although it is situated 1,000 miles inland. It is at Montreal that the St. Lawrence Seaway begins, allowing ships, after a 1,200-mile journey, to reach the Great Lakes. It was the French king, Louis XIV who made possible the building of the harbour, when he granted the Society of the New World a strip of land measuring some twenty acres along the banks of the river.

Montreal. Right: A detail of the "biosphere", the American pavilion in the Universal Exhibition of 1967, and an overall view of the Exhibition site. Below: two views of the fairground "La Ronde" and the old French pavilion of the Exhibition.

Winter... Two inhabitants skiing along a road in Point-Senneville. Ice hockey in a poor quarter of Montreal. Right: Curious sights in Montreal: *a restaurant and a telephone booth in the Chinese quarter; a further example of old houses with outside staircases; a concrete wall brighte-* *ned up with coloured paintings and a restaurant whose name and appearance recalls the France of earlier days.*

QUEBEC, CITY OF HISTORY

How can one fail to like Quebec, which is undoubtedly one of the most beautiful cities in North America? The capital of this beautiful province gives off a perfume of Europe, which particularly impresses visitors.

Its charm lies first and foremost in the old town. Old Quebec, encircled by ramparts, represents, in fact, a historical area without equal, bearing witness to almost four centuries of history.

In 1535, Jacques Cartier came as far as the present site of the city, where Indians then lived, in a settlement called Stadacona, but it was Samuel de Champlain who founded the town in 1608. Louis Bebert and his wife Marie Rollet, who arrived in 1617, were the first French people to till the soil in New France.

Quebec developed after 1632, a date which marked the beginning of a half-century of peace between France and England. The Jesuits founded their college there in 1635, and two years later the Augustinians built what was to become *Hôtel-Dieu.* The Ursuline Convent, the Cathedral and the Seminary were all built between 1638 and 1678. The administrator Jean Talon, who arrived in 1663, developed industry, and a naval shipyard, a brewery, a tannery, as well as shoe and hat factories, sprang up in the low town. Thanks to the settlers brought in by Jean Talon, different parishes and Seigniories were established in the region.

When hostilities were reopened between France and England, an English fleet, commanded by Sir William Phipps, demanded the surrender of the town in 1690. Governor Frontenac's reply to Phipps' messenger was immediate: "Tell your master that I will reply to him through the mouth of my canons." And the English fleet left without insisting further.

In 1690, Quebec had only 1,500 inhabitants and only 2,300 twenty-five years later, but its geographical situation made it strategically and economically important.

In the 18th century, the first walls of the town were erected, yet it was a badly-protected town that James Wolfe made his attack on in 1759, continuing his bombardment for the whole of the summer, and destroying nearly all the buildings. On 13th September, thanks to a carefully-organized plan, Wolfe managed to arrange 5,000 men on the Heights of Abraham. Instead of withdrawing behind the fortification, the Marquis of Montcalm undertook a sortie, Wolfe allowed the French to advance and ordered his men to fire at close range. The battle lasted no longer than twenty minutes, and the two leaders, Wolfe and Montcalm, gave their lives on the battlefield. France had just lost a battle with far-reaching consequences. The following year, Lévis, commander of the French troops, began in his turn the siege of Quebec, occupied by the English. The final result depended on the arrival of the first reinforcements, and it was an English frigate which appeared on the scene. This episode marked the end of the French regime, confirmed by the Treaty of Paris of 1763.

American troops, commanded by General Montgomery and Colonel Arnold, failed in an attempt to seize control of the city in 1775. It was after this incident that the present fortifications saw the light of day, but Quebec has never since suffered another siege.

The change of regime considerably altered the inhabitants' way of life. since both the laws and the units of measurements were modified, not to mention the architecture and, of course, the fact that the English language became predominant.

In 1860, the English, who controlled the economy of the town, represented only 40% of the population. However, confronted with serious economic problems, they decided (a pleasant surprise for the French) to move further west, and Quebec became a French town again. Today, 96% of the 400,000 inhabitants of this city and its surroundings speak French.

Quebec. **One of the town gates and the Place d'Armes.**

The Château Frontenac, a general view. A self-explicit sign and a building in the Old Town. The Dufferin Terrace.

OLD QUEBEC: THE HIGH TOWN

The ramparts which surround the High Town of Quebec form a belt of almost three miles. If one begins one's visit to Old Quebec at the Saint-Jean Gate (1839), one will first go up *Rue d'Auteuil,* with its own special charm, especially in

the upper part of it where the coloured houses are clustered together one beside the other. On the way up, one will pass two other gates, the Kent Gate (1879) and the Saint-Louis Gate (1873).

Towards the top of the road one can turn off and take the *Avenue Saint-Denis,* which leads up to an excellent observation point, with a fine panora-

mic view over Old Quebec and the Saint-Lawrence. The *Rue Saint-Louis,* which runs parallel to it is one of the most beautiful in Old Quebec, with a great many historic buildings: the *Maison Maillou* (1736), the *Maison Jacquet* (1675) and the *Maison Kent* (1648), where the Governor of Ramezay signed the declaration of capitulation of the town in 1759.

These different streets lead to the Governors' Garden, a very pleasant little park in which a number of shows are put on during the Summer. Close by, the Dufferin Terrace, which stands aloft looking down over the Saint-Lawrence, provides an excellent spot for walking, no matter what season it is. It is prolonged by the Governors' Promenade, which in its turn links up with the Heights of Abraham, along beside the Citadel, in the highest part of the town.

The Château Frontenac, a sumptuous hotel, which is impressive in size and an amazing sight with its green roofs and its numerous turrets, owes its name to Louis de Buade, Count of Frontenac, the illustrious governor of New France. It was built in 1893, and designed by a New York architect, Bruce Price. A central tower was added in 1924.

The *Place d'Armes* used to be called *La Grande Place,* then *Rond de Chaînes,* for after 1824 it was surrounded by a series of chains. Military parades were held here. Nearby stands the monument in honour of Samuel de Champlain, inaugurated in 1898.

The *Rue du Trésor,* usually thronged with tourists, is a narrow street, popular with portrait painters and for the sale of lithographies.

In the Anglican Cathedral of the Holy Trinity (1804), the first Church of England cathedral built outside the British Isles, one can see the "Royal Pew", which can only be occupied by the English sovereign, or his or her representative.

Not far from here is to be found the Ursuline Convent, founded in 1639. It has twice been destroyed by fire, but certain walls of its original buildings still remain. The second reconstruction dates from 1652. The present chapel (1902) is a copy of the first, in Louis XIV style.

Part of the basilica of Notre-Dame, a Catholic cathedral, dates from as long ago as 1647, but was destroyed during the siege of Quebec in 1759, and again in 1922, this time by fire. Close beside the cathedral is situated the seminary, founded in 1663 by the first bishop of Quebec, the Lord Bishop of Laval, whose body lies in the memorial chapel. This group of 17th-century buildings is remarkable. The sundial was installed in 1773.

Going down the *Côte de la Fabrique,* one arrives in the *Rue Saint-Jean,* the busiest street in Old Quebec. The *Rue Saint-Stanislas,* a turning on the left, leads to the Presbyterian Church of Saint Andrew (1810), with a certain charm all its own. On one side of the *Côte du Palais* stands the *Hôtel-Dieu,* and on the other side the *Parc de l'Artillerie.* This consists of a group of military buildings dating from different periods. The *Redoute Dauphine* (1712-1748), strengthened with solid buttresses, is one of the most interesting of them.

Quebec. The Ursuline Convent and the picturesque **Rue du Trésor,** *very popular with tourists. Right: names, signs and houses, which reveal the deeply-implanted French character of the city. The house at the top was the General Headquarters of Montcalm.*

OLD QUEBEC:
LA PLACE ROYALE

La Place Royale, situated in the Low Town, which can most easily be reached by climbing the Casse-Cou Steps, was in a way the cradle of New France.

It was indeed on this spot (or to be more precise, on the present site of the Church of Notre-Dame-des-Victoires) that Samuel de Champlain, in 1608, built his *"abitation",* as it was written in those days—his first permanent abode in Quebec. It served him as a fort, a residence and as a trading-post. This first dwelling, built of wood, did not resist the harshness of the climate for very long, so Champlain had a second building erected

on the same site, this time much larger. About sixty people lived here, and it was here too that Champlain died on Christmas Day 1635, at the age of 65.

Five years later, this second residence of Champlain's was converted into the *Magasin du Roi,* and surrounded by the store of the company of the *Cent-Associés,* the house of a merchant—the Master of the Chatelets—as well as the residence and chapel of the Récollets. After two decades, the lay-out of the streets was more or less the same as it is today.

The closeness of the river St. Lawrence made this situation an ideal place for merchants who traded with France and the West Indies. The richest of them had luxurious houses built, combi-

ning them into architecturally harmonious sector of the town, which was preserved until the end of the French regime.

About 1860, *La Place Royale* became a financial quarter, where branches of the different banks were opened, spoiling the earlier beauty of the area. The houses themselves were ruined by the addition of extra storeys.

In 1967, the government of Quebec province having passed a law which allowed the restoration of *La Place Royale,* all the buildings of this sector were restored to their original state and *La Place Royale,* which had for a long time been abandoned, thus became again an outstanding historic site, to which tourists flocked.

Casse-Cou Steps, today called the Cham-

plain Steps, come out into *Rue Petit-Champlain*, the most ancient street in North America. *Rue Sous-le-Port* leads as far as the *Batterie Royale*, which was built in 1691 to protect the town from enemy attacks. There were eleven canons there in 1712. About 1805, the battery was buried under warehouses.

The Church of Notre-Dame-des-Victoires (dating from 1688) is a reminder of two French victories: the victory against Philips in the year 1690, and the one against Walker in 1711. The main altar is in the shape of a fortified castle, right down to the very smallest detail. The side chapel is dedicated to Sainte-Geneviève, the patron saint of Paris.

Among the many fine buildings in *La Place Royale*, the *Maison Chevalier* (dating from 1752) should be given a special mention. It consists of three distinctly separate buildings, and now contains the very interesting Museum of Quebec Furniture.

The *Maison des Vins* has been installed in the *Maison Dumont,* built in 1689, with some magnificent vaulting. Also worth a visit amongst the other residences of character are: the *Maison Le Picard* and the outstanding *Maison Fornel* (1735), in which are displayed a good many objects discovered during the excavations carried out on the site of Champlain's *"abitation"*. Not far away from here, one can wind one's way up *Rue Saint-Pierre* and *Rue Saint-Paul.* The latter is well-known for its antique shops.

Quebec. Left: the "Casse-Cou" Staircase: it links the Low Town to the Old Town. The **Maison Chevalier,** *in the heart of the* **Place Royale.** *Below: old houses and shops in the* **Rue Paul.** *Above: the impressive plate commemorating the foundation of Quebec and a view of the* **Rue Saint-Pierre.** *Below: the Church of* **Notre-Dame-des-Victoires** *in the* **Place Royale** *and, in the centre of it, a bust of none other but Louis XIV, the Sun-King. Following pages: an interesting photo combines the* **Place Royale** *and the Château Frontenac. As for the barouche decorated with a* **fleur de lys,** *this is quite a symbol!*

THE CITADEL AND
THE HEIGHTS OF ABRAHAM

The Citadel of Quebec stands on the highest point of Cape Diamond (330 feet), which looks down over the St. Lawrence, very near Old Quebec.

A first, very rudimentary construction was put up here in 1693. It was enlarged and strengthened later, on several occasions. In 1750 the French added certain fortifications: the redoubt and the powder-house.

The present Citadel was built in 1820 by the English, under the direction of Lieutenant Colonel E.W. Durnford, of the Royal Engineers, with the agreement of the Duke of Wellington. Originally built with the purpose of resisting any possible attack from the American troops, it has, in fact, never been used for military purposes, since no invasion has ever taken place since that time. It is a construction in Vauban style, in the shape of a star, of which each point represents a bastion. The whole thing is surrounded by a moat.

English troops occupied the Citadel up until 1871, the year in which Canadian units replaced them. Today it is the garrison headquarters of the Royal 22nd Regiment. In Summer, one can attend the ceremony of the Changing of the Guard there, as well as various processions and march-pasts. In spite of the very British character of the ceremonial procedure, the orders are given in French.

The Memorial was erected in 1964, on the occasion of the fiftieth anniversary of the Royal 22nd Regiment, in order to honour the memory of its members who fell during the 1914-18 and 1939-45 wars, as well as in Korea. Its twenty-two stained-glass windows are decorated with the coats-of-arms of Canada and Quebec, as well as the shields of the Regiment and of the nineteen units which supplied it with troops in the course of these different conflicts.

The Military Museum is housed in the powder-house. It contains mementoes of the war service of the Royal 22nd Regiment, documents dating from the French regime and uniforms.

It was on the Heights of Abraham (or: the Park of the Battlefield) that the decisive battle took place on 13th September 1759 between the French troops, under the command of Montcalm, and the English troops, led by General Wolfe, a battle won by the English. A concession granted on this site in 1635 to the pilot Abraham Martin, gives an explanation of the name "Heights of Abraham". There are a number of monuments here, those to Wolfe and Montcalm amongst others, as well as plates put up to commemorate the sequence of events in the battle between the French and the English. Two of the four Martello towers, built by the English between 1804 and 1806, through fear of an American invasion, are still standing.

The Heights of Abraham, a superb stretch of grass running alongside a part of the High Town of Quebec, is a very popular spot for walks, in summer and in winter. While there is snow on the ground, a great many of the inhabitants of the old town come here for cross-country skiing. The St. Lawrence river flows just below.

Quebec. Right: the ceremony of the Changing of the Guard in front of the Citadel (English uniforms but French-Canadian guards); the majestic sweep of the St. Lawrence, seen from the Promenade des Gouverneurs; *the Château Frontenac and a general view of the Citadel, seen from the river.*

Above: a view of the vast park called "The Heights of Abraham", one of the Quebecers' favourite spots for walks. Below: a barouche, on the high ground near the Heights of Abraham. Right: the building of the National Assembly of the province of Quebec.

BEYOND THE WALLS OF QUEBEC

Nobody will regret venturing beyond the ramparts of the old town.

The *Grande-Allée*, lined with trees, begins at the Saint-Louis Gate and runs along beside the Heights of Abraham. Private hotels are dotted about here and there along this thoroughfare where the homes of wealthy folk abound, although it has also been popular with the less well-off for a good many years now, because of the opening up of a number of restaurants, bars and discotheques.

The building of the National Assembly of the province dates from 1881 and is in Renaissance style. Other buildings that surround it, modern in contrast, house the different government Ministries.

Continuing along the *Grande-Allée*, one can see, in the *Place George V*, the Military Manege (1895) with its curious green roof. *Rue Claire-Fontaine*, a turning on the right-hand side, leads to the main theatre in Quebec, inaugurated in 1970. Further on, almost on the Heights of Abraham is situated the Museum of Quebec Province, devoted mainly to Quebec art.

If one leaves Old Quebec by the Saint-Jean Gate and proceeds up *Rue Saint-Jean* towards the west, one reaches the *Saint-Jean-Baptiste* region. The atmosphere in this area—which is not at all touristic—is rather special, as its inhabitants, students and harmless eccentrics amongst them, take an active part in local affairs, particularly within the framework of the numerous cooperatives which have developed here. The streets are narrow and the houses a little old and rickety.

At Sillery, a little town on the outskirts of Quebec itself, where the residences are often sumptuous, stands the *Vieille Maison* of the Jesuits (1637), which exhibits objects from archaeological excavations.

Sainte-Foy, a residential suburb, is well-known for the University of Laval, the oldest French-speaking university in North America (1852). The present campus dates only from 1950.

The two bridges that span the St. Lawrence just outside Sainte-Foy are most impressive structures: Quebec Bridge, opened in 1917, and Pierre-Laporte Bridge, the longest suspension bridge in the whole of Canada.

An interesting visit to make is a trip to the *Grande Hermine*, the largest of Jacques Cartier's three ships, in the Cartier-Brébeuf Park. It is here that Cartier spent the winter of 1535-36.

The Low Town areas are, for the most part, somewhat poorer than those of the High Town. It is interesting to wander about in the streets here, where tourists rarely venture; one gets perhaps a better, and certainly different, view of life in the capital.

Quebec. Right, top: in the Cartier-Brébeuf Park, a replica of the Grande Hermine, *the small sailing-boat aboard which Jacques Cartier crossed the Atlantic to give Canada to France. Opposite: the flags of Quebec with their* fleurs de lys: *the colours and the emblem of old France. A shield from the* Grande Hermine. *Right: a striking contrast: old romantic barouches and motorways and flyovers...*

WINTER IN QUEBEC
THE CARNIVAL

In Quebec, the winter creates a very special atmosphere, which it is difficult to treat with indifference. When the snow falls on the old town, it takes on the mysterious air of a fairy-tale castle, an impression accentuated by the presence of the amazing Château Frontenac, which looks as if it has been created from the imagination of some eccentric old writer!

As in Old Quebec a great many of the streets are very steeply sloping, it is very often quite an achievement to keep one's balance on the snow-covered or icy pavements. People often fall, usually causing nothing more harmful than a burst of laughter from those around who have managed to keep their feet.

A curious ballet takes place on snowy days: the ballet of the snowblowers, whose job is to remove the snow. These frightening machines overwhelm one by their enormous size. Drivers, perched on top of these science-fiction inventions, direct operations. Small tracked machines clear the snow from the pavements, surprising the pedestrians as they suddenly appear behind them.

All this snow is collected in lorries which at nightfall go and tip it into the half-frozen river, close to the place where the ferry-boats cross to Lévis from. All these strange manoeuvres can be watched from the Dufferin Terrace.

The river Saint-Charles, in the lower town, is in winter turned into an endless skating-rink on which hundreds of Quebecers come to take a little exercise and air their lungs. On the Heights of Abraham, there is cross-country skiing, as has al-

ready been mentioned, and the children amuse themselves by slipping and sliding in every conceivable manner.

But in Quebec the highlight of the year is carnival time. This takes place during the month of February and is a very popular festivity, where "caribou"—a mixture of wine and spirits—flows in large quantities. An enormous snow and ice palace is built for the occasion, around which all kinds of activities take place, especially a very spectacular competition of ice sculptures. These are modelled out of huge blocks of ice and remain there as long as an unseasonable warmth in the atmosphere does not come and spoil the festivities by melting the sculptures. In the lower town, *Rue Sainte-Thérèse* has become "Carnival Street", and those who live there carve their own sculptures in ice outside their houses.

Processions of allegorical floats are followed by a vast crowd of people, in spite of temperatures which are well below zero.

The most original event of the Carnival is without any doubt the boat race for teams, between Quebec and Lévis, through the ice in the river. There was a time when the inhabitants of the two towns used to cross the river in this way.

Quebec. Winter... a "ferry-boat" on the frozen St. Lawrence, and a view of the harbour. Right: the town and the river. The inhabitants take great pleasure in walking on the river!

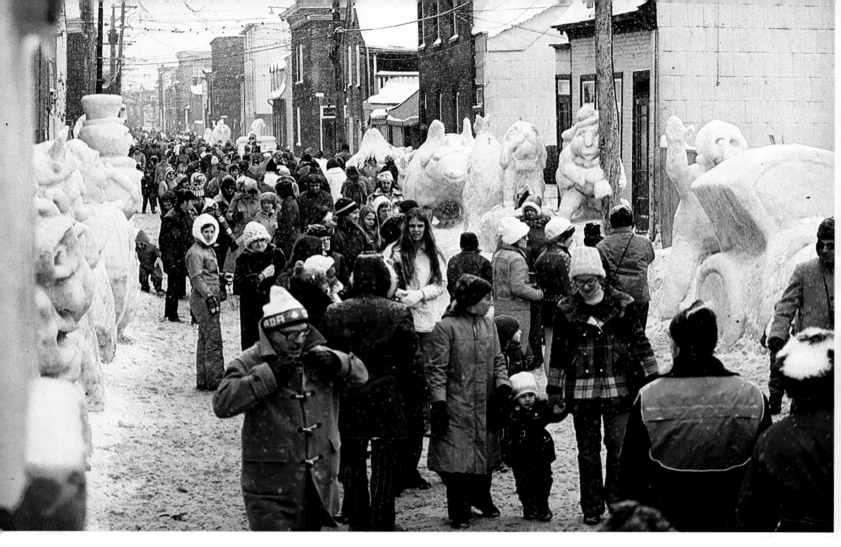

During the Quebec Carnival — the most important event of the winter — ice sculptures adorn the Rue Sainte-Thérèse *and a great ice palace is constructed. A boat race is even held on the* St. Lawrence ice! Following pages: *view over the town and its setting.*

THE ABITIBI AND THE TÉMISCAMINGUE

In 1911 a certain Edmund Horne discovered huge deposits of copper and gold in the Abitibi. But, before managing to convince businessmen of the financial interest of such a discovery, he had to make four trips in a small boat, covering a distance of over 250 miles. This region, which until then had simply been a vast hunting territory, known only to Indians and trappers, experinced at this time a real "gold rush", with fifty thousand unemployed workers coming to try their luck ! A large number of the deposits have since been exhausted but several copper, zinc and gold mines are still open.

The Abitibi ("middle water" in Algonquin) is a plain with occasional areas of high ground. It is remarkable country for hunting and fishing where that sturdy animal, the moose or American elk, is to be found. Although the moose may look docile enough, it is better not to trust him, since if he feels himself threatened, he will not hesitate to

put his head down and charge.

The usual way to reach the Abitibi is by first crossing the huge *La Vérendrye* Park (2,400 sq.miles), named in honour of the explorer Pierre Gaultier of Varennes, master of *La Vérendrye,* who discovered the Rocky Mountains.

Val-d'Or, well-named the "Gold Valley", is the gold-mining region. The first prospectors settled here in 1933, and Val-d'Or became what is called a "mushroom town". Visitors can see there the historic mining village of Bourlamaque, made up of some sixty houses, built in 1934 with pieces of grey and white spruce.

Amos was founded in 1914. The river Harricana ("the biscuit river" in Indian) runs through the town, in which can be seen, oddly enough, a cathedral in Byzantine Roman style. Near Amos lies the Algonquin reserve of Pikogan, with its picturesque chapel.

Rouyn-Noranda, the amalgamation of two distinct villages, Rouyn and Noranda, is the large industrial and commercial centre of the Abitibi.

The tall foundry chimneys stand out dark against the sky. It was on the banks of Lake Osisko (today Lake Trémoy) that Edmund Horne discovered the deposits which led to the development of the region.

To the south, the Témiscamingue, whose rolling countryside contrasts strikingly with the plain of the Abitibi. The Témiscamingue ("in deep water" in the Indian language) is an agricultural and forest-clad region, very sparsely populated, renowned for its sunsets and its pure ethereal skies.

Ville-Marie is a pleasant little town, situated on the lake-side. The panorama over the lake from the town is magnificent, especially from the chapel-grotto of Our Lady of Lourdes. Although there is very little left of the Témiscamingue fort, it is worth going a little out of one's way to visit the site alone. This fort was never used for military purposes. It was a trading-post for the whole of Western-Quebec. Very near the fort lies the "enchanted forest", which is an amazing natural phenomenon: the thuyas which make up the forest have their trunks twisted into every conceivable shape and form.

Lake Kipawa ("there is no way out"), further south, is superb, and the town of Témiscamingue, whose name is identical to that of the region itself, is set in a fine dominating position overlooking the river of the Outaouais.

Above: in Abitibi, a rapid "dancer" and a herd of Canadian moose. Left: a characteristic house of the mining village of Bourlamaqui. Right: the beautiful lake Témiscamingue.

THE OUTAOUAIS AND GATINEAU PARK

The Indian tribe of the Outaouais has given its name to the river and to this region in the west of the province of Quebec. They were the first to live in this part of the country. But the river of the Outaouais was later to prove useful also to numerous explorers as a means of venturing further and further into the interior of the continent. Jacques Cartier gave it the name of "the Great River" but it was especially Samuel de Champlain who explored all its secrets thoroughly. He even spent a winter there, in 1617, with some Indians.

The Wood Runners, which was the name given to the fur-traders who ventured in amongst the Indians, went up the river in bark canoes in order to carry on their trade with the Indians. Then in the 19th century, the timber industry began to develop, resulting in the arrival in the area of thousands of workers. The lumberjack's songs and countless legends date from this period. Nowadays, especially in Hull, a great many of the inhabitants of the Outaouais region are engaged in public service, tourism being its other main source of revenue.

Following this majestic river of the Outaouais from east to west, one comes first to Montebello, famous for its superb castle, an imposing round wooden construction which is, surprising as it may seem, a luxury hotel. From a historical point of view, however, Papineau Manor is of more interest. This was where Louis-Joseph Papineau, leader of the French-Canadian patriots' insurrection in 1837, retired to when, having been forced into exile in Paris from 1839 to 1845, he was taken in by the Duke of Montebello.

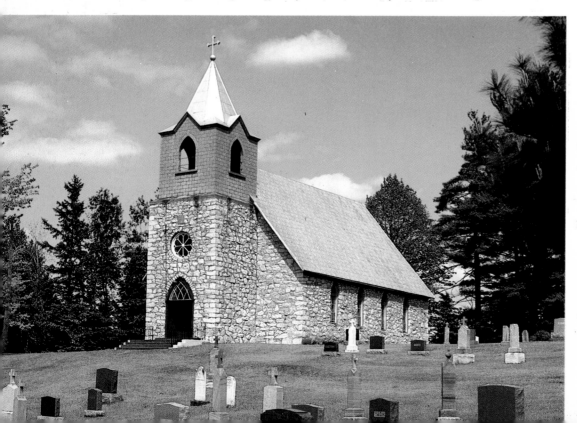

Inland from here, small roads provide a network for travelling up the valley of the *Petite-Nation* (Little Nation), whose name is the translation of "Onescharini", an Algonquin tribe. This journey across country will allow one to explore some delightful villages, such as Namur, Chénéville, Lac-Simon and Saint-André-Avellin.

To the west of Hull and Aylmer, the road leads as far as the island of the Grand-Calumet, where, of course, the Indians used to smoke the pipe of peace (*calumet* means "Indian pipe" in French), then it leads on to Fort-Coulonge, which can be proud of possessing a magnificent bridge, 425 feet long. As for the Island of Matches, where Champlain spent the winter of 1613, it takes its name from the fact that the first settlers found rushes there which they used as matches.

The two roads which rise from Hull towards the north run along the river *Gatineau* and the river Lièvre (Hare). The road beside the Gatineau passes through La Pêche, a picturesque village popular with visitors. At Lac-Sainte-Marie, the Mont-Sainte-Marie can offer countless possibilities for leisure activities, and is especially known as a ski resort. Further north lies Maniwaki, which was a former trading-post of the Hudson's Bay Company. There is a large Indian reserve there now.

The road beside the Lièvre is less busy and the country wilder. This valley was one of the first to be used by the Wood Runners. The covered bridge of Val-des-Bois measures 400 feet and is the second most important in the province.

Hull, the fifth largest town in Quebec, with almost 70,000 inhabitants, is rather different from other places, because only a bridge separates this French-speaking town from Ottawa, the capital of Canada, with an overwhelming majority of English-speakers amongst its inhabitants. This closeness to Ottawa does cause certain language difficulties. The population of Hull works mainly in the civil service, a number of federal administrative offices being situated in the town centre.

Gatineau Park, just outside the town limits, is a former Algonquin settlement. Its situation close to the town offers the inhabitants the possibility of enjoying its natural surroundings within easy reach. Paths have been marked out, which make the park a paradise for cyclists too.

It is almost impossible to count all the different varieties of the trees in the park: pine, larch, spruce, fir, thuya, walnut, poplar, beech, birch, elm, oak, maple, lime, cherry, ash, etc., all are represented there. Grouped together, they provide a wonderful combination of colours during the autumn. Animals, too, live free in the park, notable amongst them Virginian deer, wolves and beavers.

An imposing building in the heart of the park attracts the visitor's attention. This is Moorside, formerly the property of William Lyon Mackenzie King, who was for twenty-two years Prime Minister of Canada. He gathered together around his house remains of old buildings, a strange collection of ruins, set in beautiful grounds, which is not without a charm of its own.

The Outaouais. Top, left: one of the covered bridges, peculiar to Quebec. This is Fort-Coulonge Bridge. Below: the Château Montebello. Opposite: a cemetery and its chapel. Right: a clump of maples; as everyone knows, this is the national tree and the leaf has become the symbol of the country. Below: a typical little house in the middle of a wood.

THE LAURENTIDES

The Laurentides have been given the fine-sounding name of "highlands", a name which admirably defines this region situated to the north of Montreal, where little towns and villages line the road as it rises towards the north, in the direction of Mont-Laurier.

The Laurentides are part of the most ancient mountain massif in the world, formed during the Pre-Cambrian period. This massif, worn and made smooth by the weather and glacier erosion, has become a little paradise for winter sports enthusiasts from far and wide, the ski resorts having acquired a world-wide reputation.

It is to a now legendary character, the priest Father Labelle, a huge man weighing 330 lbs, that the "highlands" owe their development, between 1870 and 1890. Always having believed in the possibilities for tourism in the north, Father Labelle made the prediction that "the Laurentides will one day be the Switzerland of Canada. Foreigners will come here in large numbers from America and even from Europe". In

1870, there was not yet a single town north of Sainte-Agathe. In twenty years, the priest was to found some twenty parishes, after having covered the whole area on foot and by boat, but his most outstanding achievement was having the railway built, later to be called "the little train of the north", which ran through to Sainte-Agathe and then to Mont-Laurier. The introduction of this line completely transformed the whole area, which became popular with holiday visitors. In 1930, the Laurentides received another boost to their prosperity, thanks to the increasing popularity of skiing. Hotels were built and resorts sprang up.

The road to the north is the road for skiing. It really begins at Piedmont, after Saint-Jérôme, called "the gateway to the Laurentides". Saint-Sauveur-des-Monts is a delightful little village, which is very touristic, but whose architectural unity has somehow been preserved, in spite of the number of restaurants and cafés which have sprung up in recent years.

The well-known resorts of Mont-Gabriel and Morin-Heights lie off the main road.

Sainte-Adèle is another important ski centre, and a visit should be made to "Seraphin's village" a village which relives the life of the people of the "highlands" about 1880, through

Seraphin, the main character of a novel by Claude-Henri Grignon: *One Man and his Sin.*

Further north lie the villages of Val-Morin and Val-David, famous for its craft workshops, and Sainte-Agathe, which stands on the banks of a beautiful lake, the *lac des Sables,* and is the centre for numerous activities. The Mont-Tremblant Park is also extremely popular with visitors. With its 1,000 sq.miles, its 985 lakes and the highest summit in the Laurentides (2,600 feet), its resources seem inexhaustible. Continuing along the same road, one reaches Mont-Laurier, an important industrial centre.

The "Route des Anciens Français" is not for skiing, situated as it is to the west of Montreal and leading to the Outaouais.

Terrebonne, situated in the former territory surrendered to Sieur Daulier des Landes in 1673, is of historical interest. It became an important trading centre during the 18th century. Its mill

produced the flour used in the manufacture of the biscuits sailors took with them on their voyages.

On the island, the *île des Moulins,* four classified buildings are worth a visit: the bakery, the flour mill, the new mill and the seigniorial office.

A little to the west is to be found Saint-Eustache, which was, on 14th December 1837, the scene of a cruel episode in the history of French-Canadians. Seventy Patriots, as well as their leader, Dr. Chénier, lost their lives in an attack by the troops of the English General Colborne. Traces of cannon-ball fire are visible on the facade of the church in which the Patriots took refuge.

The Trappist monastery at Oka is renowned, since the monks have for a long time made their own cheese of excellent quality. The further one continues along the road, the more beautiful it becomes, especially in the region of Carillon and Grenville.

The Laurentides, land of mountains, forests and water, near Montreal. Left: two different views of this beautiful region. Above: a "partie" at which one enjoys maple syrup prepared on the spot. The Laurentides are also a paradise for skiers. Opposite: the holiday resort of Saint-Sauveur-des-Monts.

DE LANAUDIÈRE

This region, much less well-known than the neighbouring Laurentides, is nevertheless extremely pleasant to drive through, stopping perhaps to look at the numerous waterfalls on the way.

The area was first occupied by the Iroquois and Algonquins, and was later, in the course of the 17th century, taken over by Seigniories. About 1815, American loyalists, faithful to the British Crown, settled in the area, followed shortly afterwards by Irish Catholics, then in the 19th century by Germans and Slavs. Nowadays, De Lanaudière consists mainly of agricultural land, and produces, surprisingly enough, large quantities of tobacco.

At Berthierville, on the banks of the river, Cuthbert Chapel, dating from 1786, was the first Presbyterian church in Lower Canada. James Cuthbert, a former aide-de-camp of General Wolfe's at the battle of the Heights of Abraham, had it built after the death of his wife. The archipelago of Berthierville, made up of a large number of islands, at the end of April provides a refuge for migratory birds, ducks and bustards.

Tobacco is also grown around Saint-Thomas, and both here and in the area surrounding L'Assomption, Lavaltrie, Lenoraie, and Sainte-Mélanie one will notice little houses which are, in fact, meant for drying tobacco. The yellowish sandy soil characteristic of this part of the country has proved ideal for the production of tobacco, a discovery made about 1935, on the initiative of Friar Marie Victorin. Tobacco is harvested during the month of August. The country air, during this period, is not quite so pleasant to breathe.

Joliette is a charming little town, with a real cultural vocation, in spite of its closeness to Montreal. It was founded in 1823 by Barthélemy Joliette, a descendant of one of the discoverers of the Mississipi. Its art gallery houses, notably, a collection of Canadian paintings and sculptures, and another giving a panorama of the religious art of the province of Quebec.

A stop must be made at Rawdon, founded by American loyalists at the beginning of the 19th century, to see the Dorwin Falls, on the river Ouareau. The rock to the right of the falls resembles the shape of an Indian's head. Legend has it that it was that of a Huron who is thought to have pushed his woman companion over the edge into the abyss. The Canadiana village also at Rawdon is a historic centre, composed of about twenty houses and other buildings, reconstructing, with the help of costumes of the period, the life of last century.

Heading north, one will drive through pleasant villages, such as Sainte-Marcelline, Sainte-Mélanie and Saint-Jean-de-Matha. Between the last two villages one's attention will be caught by the impressive sight of "Les Dalles" Falls. As for Saint-Gabriel, to the east of De Lanaudière, this is an important centre for tourists. At Saint-Zénon, much further north, long staircases lead the visitor up to the Seven Falls viewpoint from which there is a marvellous panoramic view over the valley below.

Lastly, at Saint-Michel-des-Saints, a touristic little town, one cannot help but be impressed by the vast Taureau reservoir, the distant around which is no less than 435 miles.

Left: one of the numerous breathtaking waterfalls of the De Lanaudière country, and the little church of Rawdon. Right: an aerial view of the forest camp of Lake Taureau, and Lake Rond, a canoe trip, in winter.

Above: the hunting of moose is carried on from watchtowers which enable the huntsman to wait quietly and well-hidden for the arrival of this *animal, which is especially ferocious. Below: detail of the construction of a wooden chalet, and the window of another chalet. Right:* *equipped with snowshoes and overboots, the Quebecer can go for delightful walks in the deep snow.*

TROIS-RIVIÈRES

Trois-Rivières is one of the oldest towns in North America, since it was founded in 1634 by the Master of Laviolette, who was in command of a fort which stood on this spot.

Jacques Cartier had in 1535 erected a cross on the island of Saint-Quentin on the site of what is now Trois-Rivières. Eighty years later, Champlain was to set up a trading-post on the same spot.

This name of Trois-Rivières was the result of a mistake on the part of Champlain. There is, in fact, only one river, the Saint-Maurice, but as it flows around the two little islands of its delta, the islands of la Potherie and of Saint-Quentin, the river forms three channels.

Trois-Rivières was the first town in Canada to have an ironworks: the Saint-Maurice works. Established in 1730 to exploit the iron-ore in the Seigniory of Saint-Maurice, these works continued to produce iron until 1883. The remains of it can be visited, a few miles outside the town. What is left of the old furnace should be especially noted.

The town reached the height of its industrial prosperity in the middle of the 19th century, thanks to the exploitation of its forests. Nowadays, it is one of the largest centres of newsprint manufacture, as well as being a very important port.

The inhabitants of Trois-Rivières are called the "Trifluviens". The life of the town is centred on the City Hall Square and the crossroads formed by the streets of Saint-Georges, Des Forges, Royale et Notre-Dame.

In the cathedral of mock Gothic style, built in 1854, the stained glass windows by Guido Nincheri from Florence, produced in 1923, are considered to be the finest in North America. They represent litanies of the Blessed Virgin. The bell-tower is the work of Victor Bourgeau.

But it is Old Trois-Rivières to which we should give most of our attention. The Ursuline Convent in the street of the same name, the building of which was started in 1697, is in Norman style. It has been enlarged and restored on numerous occasions. Its sundial dates from 1860.

Tonnancour's House (1690) is the most ancient building in the town. The Anglican Church of St. James, of which certain parts date right back to 1699, was rebuilt in 1754. Erected by the Récollets, it was used at different times as a prison, Law Courts and Governor's Residence, before becoming a church. In *Rue Bonaventure* stands the remarkable Boucher de Niverville Manor (1729). A monument to the glory of the Master of Laviolette has been raised on the *Terrasse Turcotte*.

The Laviolette bridge, inaugurated in 1967, provides the modern image of Trois-Rivières. More than two miles long, it spans the St. Lawrence and allows access to the region of the Bois-Francs.

Trois Rivières. Left: the centre of the town with, in the background, the cathedral; the harbour, on the St. Lawrence, and the historic Ursuline Convent, with its sun-dial. Right: a ferry-boat is loading a lorry carrying wood. Below: one of the many lakes in the national park of La Mauricie nearby. Following pages: a charming view of the Saint-Maurice, which has given its name to the region.

LA MAURICIE

La Mauricie is, first and foremost, nature: innumerable lakes, the river Saint-Maurice, really magnificent, amazing waterfalls and natural parks which are a paradise for those who love peace and quite.

But La Mauricie is also Trois-Rivières, one of the oldest towns in North America, and Cap-de-la-Madeleine, a well-known place of pilgrimage.

This region has always been an industrial area. The first iron and steel works in Canada were established here as long ago as the 18th century, while sawmills were introduced to the region during the 19th century. Now, the paper represents its main source of revenue.

If one follows the road which runs along beside the St. Lawrence, from west to east, a detour to see the Sainte-Ursule Falls is without any doubt a first priority. Formed in 1663 at the time of an earthquake, which caused a difference in level of 230 feet in the bed of the Maskinongé River, they are breathtaking to see, falling with gushing force to the water below.

Lake Saint-Pierre is a widening out of the St. Lawrence, and can be admired from Pointe-du-Lac.

To the east of Trois-Rivières is Cap-de-la-Madeleine, a centre for pilgrimage since the time when three witnesses saw the eyes of the statue of the Virgin Mary move, in the church built in 1714 and dedicated to Notre-Dame-du-Rosaire. An enormous basilica, octagonal in shape, has been erected near the sanctuary.

At Batiscan, the former presbytery of the Jesuits (1696) is well-preserved. La Pérade owes its reputation to fishing under the ice, which is carried on throughout the winter. This fishing for "the little fish of the gutter" (small cod called "poula-mons") involves the setting-up of a whole village

of huts on the ice.

Taking the roads which lead up towards the north, one first comes to Shawinigan, an industrial town whose waterfalls are particularly beautiful. Grand-Mère owes its name to a rock which looks like the head of an old woman, called Kokomis (grandmother) by the Indians. The famous rock had to be moved right into the town-centre. In order to do this, the rock first had to be cut into several pieces, all numbered, so that they could be put together again.

Standing perched on a cliff, Grandes-Piles is a pretty village which looks down over the Saint-Maurice river. During last century the village was a landing-place for the unloading of the provisions and equipment necessary for the lumberjacks working in the north.

The park of La Mauricie, with its countless lakes, is superb. A tour of the park can easily be made by means of a well-laid out walk, where belvederes allow visitors to admire the landscape. One of the lakes in the park, Lake Wapizagonke, is without doubt one of the most beautiful in the province of Quebec.

Continuing towards the north, along the Saint-Maurice river in magnificent surroundings, one will reach the Saint-Maurice reserve, offering a natural setting similar to that of the La Mauricie park. To the north of the area, the little town of La Tuque lives off the pulp and paper industry. It is named after a mountain which bears the shape of a woollen Quebec bonnet called a "tuque".

Left: wood is the wealth of this part of the country. It floats down the Saint-Maurice (top), crosses a dam (middle) and arrives at the works. Above: a little snowy road near Trois Rivières; trout-fishing on the frozen Le Milieu river and, a folkloric scene in a village.

LE SAGUENAY

Le Saguenay is the name of a whole region, but it is first and foremost a majestically flowing river, a real fjord, which has an average width of about 650 yards, and is 65 miles long. The hills that surround it reach a height of 1,500 feet at certain places. Its name comes from the Indian "Sakini", meaning "where the water runs out". The source of the river is Lake Saint-Jean, and it flows out into the St. Lawrence at Tadoussac.

Jacques Cartier had seen the mouth of the river, bur had not gone up it. It was Champlain that made his way up it, reaching Tableau. In 1647, Father Jean de Quen explored it as far as Chicoutimi, before discovering Lake Saint-Jean.

Le Saguenay and Lake Saint-Jean were for a long time part of the "kingdom of Saguenay", a territory that belonged by right to the King of France. In 1838, at the time of the foundation of the Twenty-One Society, whose purpose was to take part in lumbering, the clearing of the land began.

This Saguenay region, in which Chicoutimi and Jonquière are the two largest towns, has always lived off the fur trade, lumbering and paper manufacturing. Today, there are a number of power stations to be found here, and one of the largest aluminium works in the world.

Following the two banks of the Saguenay means a journey of about 185 miles. Villages are few and far between. If one sets off from Tadoussac along the north bank road, one follows the river Sainte-Marguerite, overlooked by sheer rocky cliffs. To see the river Saguenay, one must go as far as Sainte-Rose-du-Nord, a very pretty village. It used to be called "the women's descent", since Indian women went to this spot to meet the men on their return from their fishing trips. The little white church where the pews are made of ash-wood, and the altar of old tree stumps, should be noted.

The small village of Saint-Basile-de-Tableau, clustered at the top of a cliff, is interesting and it is worth making a little detour to see it. There is complete peace and quiet here, and the view over the Saguenay is superb. Its little red and white chapel adds a romantic note.

Jonquière, situated to the west of Chicoutimi, is an industrial town, with the aluminium works mentioned above. Shipshaw bridge is the first in the world to have been entirely constructed in aluminium.

Coming back towards the St. Lawrence, by the south bank of the Saguenay, one will first pass through La Baie, another industrial town, set on the bay of the "Ha! Ha!". Its vast harbour installations are most impressive.

From Rivière-Eternité it is possible to walk as far as Cape Trinité (1,400 feet), from whose summit the panorama is amazing. A statue of the Virgin Mary has been erected high up above the river at this spot. Lastly, Anse-Saint-Jean is a charming village, where one of the rare covered bridges of the area is to be found.

Above: Eternity Bay and its impressive rocky cliffs. Right, top: the pretty little village of Ste-Rose-du-Nord, beside the Saguenay river. Opposite: a view of Chicoutimi; this is the most important town in the region. Following pages: Bagoiville, on the Saguenay river.

CHICOUTIMI

The name of Chicoutimi comes from "Esh-ko-timiou", meaning in the Indian language "up to where it is deep". The river Saguenay is indeed navigable from its estuary right up to this very place.

A trading-post and a mission settlement had been established on the present site of he town, as far back as 1676, but the real date for the foundation of Chicoutimi was 24th August 1842, when a young builder of Scottish origin, Peter McLeod, settled there with about twenty other men and opened up a sawmill, worked by the water from the river Moulin. The following year he had another larger one built, on the river Chicoutimi.

Two settlements then developed around each sawmill, a church was put up between the two and Chicoutimi soon became a town.

It has now spread along both banks of the river Saguenay, made up of three municipalities: Chicoutimi, Chicoutimi-North and Rivière-du-Moulin.

The old pulp-mill can be visited, four imposing buildings, bearing witness to its origins. The site has become a lively spot where, in fine weather, musicians and actors perform.

Very near the old pulp-mill, one little house, lost in a very ordinary street, deserves a visit. It has, in fact, been entirely painted — both inside and outside — by its owner, Arthur Villeneuve.

He took his inspiration from the history of the town, legends from the region and biblical scenes. After this piece of work, Arthur Villeneuve's fame spread well beyond Chicoutimi, since he is now considered in Canada to be an excellent naïve painter.

The Saguenay-Lac-Saint-Jean Museum is devoted to regional history. Several rooms are taken up by a reconstruction of life last century, and its collection of Indian objects is one of the most remarkable in the province of Quebec.

The cruises on the Saguenay leave from Chicoutimi: it is well worth going on one during the summer. If, on the other hand, you are in Chicoutimi in the winter, in February, it is traditional carnival time that will entertain you for about ten days.

The Chicoutimi carnival is thought to be the most authentic in the province. The inhabitants dress up in costumes of the 19th century. Traditional dancing and trials of strength are the order of the day.

Starting the tour of the lake from the south, one passes through Métabetchouan ("current which is concentrated before flowing into the sea") in the Montagnais language. The Indians from twenty different nations met not far from here at the first trading-post established in the region. The beautiful neo-Gothic church in pink granite is remarkable. At Desbiens, one must visit the cave, "The Fairy's Hole", which is 250 feet deep.

But it is the ghost village of Val-Jalbert that deserves a longer stay. Its inhabitants — about 1,000 people — used to work in former days in a paper-mill established at the beginning of the century by a certain Damase Jalbert. Completely abandoned for 35 years, Val Jalbert has now become a favourite spot for walkers. Its houses — about sixty in all — do have a certain charm. The Cuiatchouan Falls ("place where one catches many white fish"), 240 feet high, are superb.

Roberval was the first parish to be established on the shores of the lake (1855). It is named after the Master of Roberval, first viceroy of Canada, who tried in 1543 to reach "the kingdom of Saguenay". Roberval is the arrival-point of the famous international swimming race across the Lake Saint-Jean, held each year in August.

The Montagnais reserve of Pointe-Bleue was founded in 1856. The museum retraces the history of the Montagnais Indians. The Montagnais language at one time almost disappeared, but is now officially taught.

The zoo of Saint-Félicien is a remarkable one. A miniature train takes visitors round while the animals remain at liberty. It is at Dolbeau that the blueberry aperitif is made. Blueberries, fruit which look like large bilberries, are the source of a considerable revenue for Lac-Saint-Jean. As for the Trappist monastery of Mistassini, founded in 1892 and turned into an abbey in 1935, they produce there some very good chocolate.

The French writer Louis Hémon, author of *Maria Chapdelaine,* has made the village of Péribonka famous. He stayed there in 1912 and took his inspiration from certain of the inhabitants in creating his characters. There is a museum in the village devoted to him.

Left: wooden houses in an abandoned village of the Val Jalbert and an Indian camp in the Mistassini Park. Below: the Quebec Province Museum at Lake Saint-Jean. Right: Lake Saint-Jean, seen from the falls in the river Quiatchouane.

LAC-SAINT-JEAN

The Lac-Saint-Jean region is famous in the province for its hospitality. This is an additional reason for making a tour of the lake which has given its name to the region.

The settlement of this territory really began in the middle of the 19th century. Agricultural and dairy products provided the inhabitants with their main source of revenue at that time.

In 1870 a fire destroyed almost all the cultivated land, but this did not discourage the pioneers, who continued to clear the land.

The Indians called Lac-Saint-Jean "Pie-kouagami" meaning "the flat lake". The *ouanani-che,* which is fished in the lake, is a fresh-water salmon, which can reach a weight of as much as 11 lbs and a length of three feet, and is well-known for its fighting spirit.

Alma is an industrial town, with a hydro-electric power-station, a pulp and paper mill and an aluminium works.

THE REGION OF CHARLEVOIX

Situated at less than an hour's journey from Quebec, the region of Charlevoix is indubitably one of the areas most preferred by Quebecers. The countryside there is extremely beautiful, whether it be along the St. Lawrence, where breathtaking panoramas succeed each other or in the interior, in the *"rangs"*, where one can discover peaceful villages.

The first settlers came here during the 18th century. As reminders of their time there, a number of houses, manors and mills still remain. During the 19th century, rich Americans and Canadians took over this area, which became a much-sought-after holiday region.

Now, one can never tire of touring Charlevoix, whose welcoming organization is exceptional. Its many country inns are, in addition, renowned for the quality of their cooking.

It is at Saint-Tite-des-Caps that the region really begins. Then one passes through a beautiful forest of conifer trees before reaching Baie-Saint-Paul, a small town situated on the shore of a magnificent bay, in the shadow of a dominating mountain. Baie-Saint-Paul, a village that has been inhabited since as long ago as 1678, was for a long time the only village of any size in the whole region. A number of artists and craftsmen have taken up residence in the village, whose setting inspires all kinds of artistic creation.

Starting from Baie-Saint-Paul, one can tour the *"rangs"* of the Charlevoix region and pass through, amongst other villages, Saint-Urbain, Notre-Dame-des-Monts and Sainte-Agnès, in beautiful countryside. It is at Clermont that one of the most famous Quebec personalities was born: Alexis the Trotter. His real name was Alexis Lapointe, but from a very early age he took to imitating horses, to such an extent that he used to run in the country, whinnying as he did so and grazing in the grass in the fields! He managed, amongst other exploits, to beat the boat which linked Pointe-au-Pic to Chicoutimi, as well as the best horse in the vicinity!

The road that runs along the river between Baie-Saint-Paul and La Malbaie, however, delights the tourist even more than the "rangs" road. From les Eboulements, after, going down a steep hill, one reaches Saint-Joseph-de-la-Rive, from where ferry-boats allow one to cross to the island of les Coudres. Jacques Cartier himself gave it this name in 1535, as it was covered with nut-trees — or "coudriers" in old French. It was on this island that, on 6th September 1535, the first Mass was celebrated in New France.

Taking to the road again, one must, before passing through the pretty little village of Sainte-Irénée, make a detour in the direction of the very small Cap-aux-Oies, huddled on the edge of the water. At Pointe-au-Pic, one of the most important holiday centres in Charlevoix, the huge Richelieu Manor is a luxury hotel. The little town of La Malbaie owes its name to a misfortune which befell Samuel de Champlain,who, in 1608, wanted to anchor his ship in this bay but found he had gone aground on a band of clay the following morning.

Further north, one reaches Cap-à-l'Aigle and, by means of another slight detour, the enchanting village of Port-au-Persil, which one might be unfortunate enough to miss if one is not careful. Near Saint-Siméon, the Forest Education Centre, "Les Palissades" is situated in an impressive setting, in the midst of magnificent rocky cliffs. At Baie-Sainte-Catherine, the last village in the region, Champlain signed the treaty of alliance with the Hurons, the Algonquins and the Montagnais, against the Iroquois, in 1603.

Left: evening light on the "Great Lake" in the Côte de Charlevoix, a view of Saint-Siméon, a Forest Education Centre, and the former Governors' residence, or Richelieu Manor, today a luxury hotel. Above: the river Sainte-Anne-du-Nord. Right: a villa in La Malbaie, a holiday centre.

CÔTE-NORD AND LOWER CÔTE-NORD

The Côte-Nord (North Coast) region, between Tadoussac and Sept-Iles, is first and foremost a road along the north bank of the St. Lawrence, which stretches more than 250 miles. It is also the road of the great dams, built on the river Manicouagan and on the Outardes too. And lastly, it is a hinterland dotted with lakes, which are the delight of fishermen, and where forest are thick and plentiful.

Vikings then Basque fishermen and, of course, explorers from Europe, all came to this coast. The Montagnais, of the Algonquin race, were the first to live on the North Coast. Now, exploitation of the forest represents the most certain source of revenue for the region.

No-one can remain insensitive to the beauty of the setting of Tadoussac. Situated at the mouth of the Saguenay, this village was one of the first settlements in America. In fact, Pierre Chauvin built there the first house put up by the French in Canada. This was in 1599. The reconstruction recalling this event can be visited. The delightful chapel of Tadoussac (1747) is the oldest of its kind in America.

Near Grandes-Bergeronnes, ovens once used by Basque fishermen to extract the oil from "sea-wolves"—seals—that they caught in this region, have been discovered. It is from Grandes-Bergeronnes that excursions are arranged so that visitors can admire the blue whales that disport themselves in the St. Lawrence.

Further north, a detour should be made as far as the river, to reach the little St. Anne's Chapel at Ilets-Jérémie. This is a reconstruction of a sanctuary first built in 1735.

There is a Montagnais reserve to be found at Bersimis, belonging to the Betsiamite tribe. The name of Papinachois, the following village, comes from the name of another Indian tribe and means "I like to laugh a little". Lying between the Outarde and Manicouagan rivers is the peninsula of Manicouagan, with several villages and some beautiful sandy beaches.

Hauterive and Baie-Comeau are, with Sept-Iles, the main administrative and commercial centres in this North Coast region. Baie-Comeau is a sea port in deep water.

It is here that one can take the road leading to the large hydro-electric power-stations, Manic 2, Manic 3 and Manic 5. The Manic 5 station is the most powerful of the whole complex. Its vaulted dam with its huge buttresses is a most impressive sight. More than 8,000 workmen were engaged on its construction.

Setting off again towards the north, along the river, one will find that the villages become fewer and farther between. At Pointe-des-Monts, slightly off the main road, stands one of the oldest lighthouses in Canada, dating from 1830.

Port-Cartier is the port into which some of the largest ore ships put in. A railway links Gagnon, in the north, to the heart of the mining country.

Sept-Iles, the largest town in Côte-Nord, has developed since 1950 because of the iron mines in the area. Its deep-water harbour is the second most important in Canada for the quantity of goods handled. As early as 1535, Jacques Cartier had noticed the presence of seven little islands at the entrance to the bay. A museum installed in an old trading-post retraces the history of the Montagnais Indians. During the month of May, one can observe an extraordinary phenomenon, the "rolling" of the *caplans*. The fish, closely related to the smelt, approach the shores in tens of thousands in order to reproduce, then they run aground. The river becomes a seething silver mass, and at this period the *caplans* can be fished out in handfuls from the water.

Amazing landscapes and the feeling of being away from it all, that is what the Lower Côte-Nord region has to offer. Ample time is required for discovering the area, for a long time not very well known even by the people of Quebec, but it is impossible to leave it without having been completely enchanted by so much beauty.

The trip by boat is unforgettable, with frequent glimpses of whales. But a road now links a number of the small villages on the Lower Côte-Nord. They can also be reached by plane, which is often the only means of transport available in these regions in winter.

The cascade on the river Manitou, 113 feet high, is, without doubt the most beautiful in the Côte-Nord area. A viewpoint, just before Sheldrake, looks down over the sea from a height of 330 feet. It is an ideal spot from which to observe whales.

Further on, after Rivière-au-Tonnerre, Magpie, Rivière-Saint-Jean and Longue-Pointe (where there is a fine Amerindian Church) stands Mingan. The name comes from a Basque word "Min-Gain" meaning "tongue", referring, in this case, to à tongue of sand.

The Mingan archipelago is the main focal point of interest in the Lower Côte-Nord and without doubt one of the most important in the whole of Quebec. This archipelago consists of 23 islands and a dozen or so smaller islands, spread over a distance of some 50 miles. On some of the islands, there are to be found dry-stone ovens and fragments of terra-cotta pipes which were used by the Basque fishermen for extracting whale-oil. But most surprising of all are the

numerous natural monoliths which sometimes reach a height of as much as 50 feet. Worn away over the centuries by the sea, these rocks, which stand on three slender pedestals, are called "flower-pots" or "nice old women" by the inhabitants of the region. Certainly, if one is anywhere in the vicinity it would be a great pity to miss visiting it.

Havre-Saint-Pierre is a small town which used to be called Pointe-aux-Esquimaux. It was founded in 1857 by fishermen from the Islands of the Madeleine.

The island of Anticosti is 140 miles long, 35 miles wide and the distance all round it is 300 miles. Henri Menier, the French chocolate manufacturer, was its owner from 1895 to 1926, then it belonged to the government of the province of Quebec, which turned it into a reserve for the protection of the animal life.

Along the coast, after Havre-Saint-Pierre, the inhabitants of the villages and hamlets live by cod-fishing and lobster-catching.

Founded by the Acadians, Natashquan is one of the most interesting villages. Its name comes from the Moutascouan Indian word used for a successful bear-hunt. The *"galet"* on the beach is a collection of little fishermen's huts. Three or four miles away there is an Indian reserve. At Blanc-Sablon, at the end of the trip, a ferry-boat returns visitors to Newfoundland.

Top, left: general view of the little town of Tadoussac. Above: a ferry-boat which bears the name of "Trans Saint-Laurent". Opposite: the largest concrete dam in the world, at the power-station of "Manic 5".

THE RICHELIEU VALLEY AND THE SOUTH BANK

This region is packed with history, containing a vast number of reminders of the past, especially along the River Richelieu.

Samuel de Champlain followed this river in 1609 on his way to fight against the Iroquois. Later, as the Iroquois took to attacking the French communities at regular intervals, fortifications were put up all along the riverside.

At the end of the 18th century, the region was the scene of a number of skirmishes between the French and the English, then between the English and the Americans. The Rebellion of the Patriots, French Canadians who in 1837-38 rose against the central power dominated by English-speakers, was limited almost entirely to the Richelieu valley.

Nowadays, this agricultural area is a much-appreciated holiday centre. It is in the Canadian Railway Museum at Saint-Constant that the lar-gest collection of railway equipment in North America is to be found. On the site of what is now La Prairie, a trading-post was set up in 1673, where several Indian tribes lived together. The first Canadian railway line was built in 1836, between La Prairie and Saint-Jean. Horses had to be called in to help the locomotive to start on the day of the inauguration of the line. The historical background of La Prairie is most interesting, and the area can be covered on foot. Especially worth noticing are the Maison Brossard (17th century) and the Church of the Nativity (1841). At Saint-Lambert, a favourite pastime of the inhabitants is that of watching the boats pass through the locks.

Longueuil, a town of some 120,000 inhabitants is the fourth in size in the province of Quebec. The Electricity Museum is the only one of its kind in Canada, and is worth a visit. The Seigniory in which it is situated was granted to Charles LeMoyne in 1657, and he gave it the name of Longueuil, after his home village in Normandy. One of LeMoyne's sons, Iberville, discovered the Mississippi. Boucherville, founded in 1668 (which makes it one of the most ancient localities in the province) is the proud possessor of a number of fine old residences, including the Manor House of François-Pierre Boucher (1672).

At Verchères, Madeleine de Verchères, only fourteen years old, and helped by only five men, resisted the Iroquois for eight days in 1692. She was one of the first French-Canadian heroines.

The naval shipyards of Sorel provide work for a large proportion of the inhabitants of the region. The centre of the town is at Royal Square (1783). The Governor's House (1800) was formerly the summer residence of the Governor-General of Canada and of visiting English princes. A trip can be made from here to the islands of Sainte-Anne-de-Sorel, where they serve as a speciality *la gibelotte,* a sort of soup with fish and vegetables.

It is from Sorel that one should begin exploring the banks of the Richelieu. One can pass easily from one side of the river to the other, thanks to small ferry-boats, which come when they are called for.

Saint-Ours, a village founded in 1650, is the oldest in the region. It was there on 7th May 1837 that the Patriots passed a vote in favour of a declaration of war against the central authority. Eight hundred of them, led by Dr. Nelson, won an important victory over the government troops at Saint-Denis. At Saint-Charles, on 23rd October 1837, 25,000 people, supporters of the Patriots,

Above and opposite: the graceful meandering of the Richelieu, not far from Montreal, and the canal of the Moine, at the Iles de Ste-Anne-de-Sorel. Right, top: the Richelieu, at Belœil. Opposite: the interior courtyard and the entrance of Fort Lennox, on the Ile aux Noix.

carried a number of resolutions, inspired by the American Declaration of Independence, which incited the inhabitants to revolt. Unfortunately, on 25th November, two days after the conflict at Saint-Denis, the Patriots suffered a cruel defeat at Saint-Charles.

Saint-Marc is a village which is very popular with holiday visitors, with some excellent restaurants. Beloeil is also a residential town, situated in a magnificent setting. Old Beloeil, a remarkable collection of buildings, is a very lively, busy place. Inns, cafés and bars all have their place there. Opposite Beloeil stands the impressive Mount Saint-Hilaire, its slopes covered with apple-trees. In the village of the same name, special attention should be given to the Rouville-Campbell Manor House (1832), the only Tudor-style house in Canada.

Further east, Saint-Hyacinthe, on the river Yamaska, is an important agricultural centre, in a region where apple-trees abound and provide the main crop of the area.

Richelieu is a pretty, quiet village. Opposite is Chambly, where one should not miss the Church of St. Stephen (1820), nor, more important still, Chambly Fort, one of the historical highlights of the valley. Built in wood in 1665, in order to protect the French settlers from raids by the Iroquois, it was rebuilt in stone in 1709. But the French abandoned it to the English on 1st September 1760, which allowed them to go on and conquer Montreal.

At Saint-Jean, the main centre of the valley, there is the interesting Historical Museum of the Upper Richelieu to see. This is the starting-point for excursions up as far as Fort Lennox, which was built in 1759 by the French, but was taken by the English troops a few days before Fort Chambly, although the 1,400 Frenchmen, under the command of Bougainville, resisted General Haviland's English soldiers for about ten days.

To the south lie peaceful little roads, and at Hemmingford one will find a safari park where one can drive around amongst the animals, which

can wander about freely in the park. The road then continues through orchards.

Not far from Howick is situated the centre of interpretation of the Battle of Châteauguay, where on 26th October 1813 Charles-Michel de Salaberry repulsed the American army on their way to Montreal. It is best to visit Salaberry-de-Valleyfield in the summer, as it is then that international regattas are held there.

There is a historical park at Coteau-du-Lac, where a fort built in 1779 previously stood: the garrisons on the spot kept watch over the traffic on the St. Lawrence.

A stop at Vaudreuil to visit the Regional Historical Museum should be followed by a detour to visit Perrot Island and to take a walk around another historical park, the Pointe-du-Moulin Park, with its old windmill (dating from 1705) and the miller's house.

On the way back to Montreal one will pass through the Iroquois' reserve of Caughnawaga ("there are rapids" in Iroquois), founded in 1667.

L'ESTRIE AND SHERBROOKE

L'Estrie, or the Eastern Cantons, is one of the most original areas in the province, although it is not as well-known as la Gaspésie, Charlevoix or the Laurentides. Its originality comes from the mixture of English and French cultures, which makes it possible for the traveller to pass on the same circular tour through English-speaking villages and through others where French-speakers are in the majority.

The Abenaquis, from the Indian family of the Algonquins, were the first inhabitants of l'Estrie, a region which was only settled in towards the end of the 18th century, when American loyalists, faithful to the British Crown, went into exile because of the War of Independence. Then French Canadians settled in their turn in the Eastern Cantons and today 85% of the Estrians are French-speaking.

Coming from the direction of Montreal, the first place one comes to is Granby, an industrial town, known throughout Quebec as much for its gastronomy—excellent restaurants abound there—as for its zoological gardens. South of Granby, Cowansville is a small town with red brick houses, typical examples of loyalist architecture. Near the American frontier one will pass through delightful English-type villages, lost amongst the orchards: Dunham, Stambridge-East (with its 1830 Cornell mill, which now houses a regional museum) and Frelighsburg.

Sutton is one of the most important skiing resorts in the province, very popular with Mon-

lofty situation over the magnificent Lake Memphrémagog. Visitors can attend offices with Gregorian chanting by the monks.

Magog, a pretty little old town, which attracts a good many tourists, is the arrival-point for the international swimming race across Lake Memphrémagog, a race of more than thirty miles, which starts from Newport in the United States.

Mount Orford is an impressive mountain, on whose slopes there are good facilities for many sporting activities, especially Alpine and cross-country skiing. The panoramic view from the summit (2,640 feet) is magnificent.

Sherbrooke (with a population of about 90,000) is the most important industrial and commercial centre in l'Estrie, but it is also the seat of a widely-renowned university.

The town stretches over undulating country surrounded by a number of hills. It is possible to ski in the very centre, on the slopes of Mount Bellevue, very near the university. It is the Old North of the town that provides its main architectural attraction—a number of interesting examples of Victorian houses.

The *Champ de Mars* is a grassy rectangle, surrounded by solid good-class houses.

trealers. As for Lake Brome, this is particularly well-known for its ducks, a much-appreciated gastronomic speciality.

Towards the east, the Abbey of Saint-Benoît-du-Lac, of the congregation of Saint-Pierre-de-Solesme, is an outstanding building, for which the architect Dom Bellot was responsible. The abbey is in pink granite and looks down from its

Left: an old mill, at Stanbridge-Est, today converted into a museum, and the provincial park of Mount Orford. Right, top: a round barn — one of the particularities of L'Estrie. Above: the little Lake Lyster. Opposite: canoeing on Lake Brompton.

river tumble down with tumultuous force. Then there is Sainte-Marie, with its 1856 church, whose bell-tower reaches a height of 230 feet, and Lacroix House (1793). The countryside around Vallée-Jonction is typical of La Beauce. Dairy farms are numerous. At Saint-Joseph; more falls on the river Chaudière. At Beauceville one can try maple-syrup, as this town is famous for the production of it. The covered bridge of Notre-Dame-des-Pins must not be missed. Measuring 514 feet, it is the longest in Quebec province. Saint-Georges is the commercial centre of La Beauce. The *parc des Sept-Chutes* is a very popular spot for walks. Along the river it is no longer quite la Beauce but the road, which is part of la Gaspésie, runs through some very beautiful scenery.

The view over Quebec from Lévis is unique. And then there is Cap-Saint-Ignace (Gamache Manor dating from 1744) and L'Islet-sur-Mer, "the land of sailors", and especially of Captain Bernier who, in the name of Canada, took possession of the Arctic islands en 1909.

Saint-Jean-Port-Joil owes its reputation to its wood-carvings. One can find works of exquisite craftsmanship and others of more commercial value... The church built in 1779 is a masterpiece.

Lastly, at Saint-Roch-des-Aulnaies, a visit must be paid to the Seigniory of the Aulnaies, which is very well preserved, with its Manor House (1850) and its windmill.

THE CENTRE DU QUEBEC REGION, BOIS-FRANCS, LA BEAUCE

The two main towns in the Centre du Québec region are Drummondville and Nicolet. For the region of Bois-Francs they are Victoriaville and Plessiville. The fertile soil of these two areas has favoured the development of dairy production and the cultivation of various crops.

Drummondville is an old industrial town. This very interesting village of the Quebec of earlier times gives the visitor a good idea of what life was like for French Canadians last century. The Parc des Voltigeurs is a pleasant place for walks, and is only about 3.5 miles from the town

first half of the 18th century. In 1775, the inhabitants of La Beauce helped the American troops, commanded by Colonel Arnold, against the English. The English army, as a reprisal for it, occupied La Beauce for eight years.

Today, the region is particularly well-known for the sap-houses where, with the family or with friends, one can enjoy the satisfaction of a huge meal, in which maple-syrup is the main ingredient.

The traditional route through La Beauce follows the river Chaudière, famous for its tendency to flood when the breaking up of the ice is especially abundant.

First there is Charmy; the falls and the

Left: the covered bridge of Notre-Dame-des-Puis, in Beauce. The gathering of the maple sap, from which the famous syrup is made; the mighty Montmorency falls.

centre. Also interesting to visit: Trent Manor (1836) and its outbuildings, and the Anglican Church of St. George's (1855).

Abinaquis live in the Indian reserve of Odanak, where one can visit a museum devoted to them. Each year, in July, the "Pow-Wow" takes place. This is a great time of festivities, with traditional songs and dances being the order of the day.

Nicolet is proud to possess a very fine modern cathedral, whose enormous stained-glass window was designed by the local artist Jean Charland.

Victoriaville is the industrial centre of the Bois-Francs area. Many furniture manufacturers have opened up factories there. Plessiville is at the heart of a region proud of its maple groves.

From Bois-Francs, one can go on to la Beauce, one of the most attractive regions situated south of the capital. Having been isolated for so long, la Beauce possesses a very definite character of its own. The people of la Beauce have a reputation for enjoying good living. Their language is very vivid, very racy.

French Seigniories settled there during the

CÔTE DE BEAUPRÉ

The coast from Quebec to Cape Tourmente is called the Côte de Beaupré, and stretches for a distance of about 30 miles to the east of the capital.

It deserves a leisurely visit to see the large number of 17th-century dwellings. Indeed, it is on this coast, with its very fertile soil that the first New French farmers settled, in about 1640.

It is better not to take the main road along the river, but rather the road, called *Avenue Royale,* which winds along, set back slightly, sometimes at the foot and sometimes at the top of the cliff that overhangs the river.

A first halt must be made at the Montmorency Falls, 280 feet high (one and a half times the height of the Niagara Falls, though not nearly as wide). Breathtaking! It was Samuel de Champlain who gave the Falls their name in 1603, in honour of Charles de Montmorency, viceroy of New France.

All along the road, the traditional houses of French Canada, built of stone, with low doors and narrow windows, line the route. At Courville on 31st July 1759, a battle took place in which the French crushed the troops of General Wolfe. Boischatel and L'Ange-Gardien are two more most pleasant villages. Château-Richer (1640) can boast stone houses three hundred years old which have been preserved intact.

The road then goes on to the sanctuary of Sainte-Anne-de-Beaupré. More than a million people make a pilgrimage here each year. An earlier wooden chapel was built here in 1658. During its construction, a miraculous healing took place. The first stone church (1676) was used for two centuries. A first basilica (1887) was destroyed by fire in 1922 and was replaced four years later by the present huge basilica in Neo-Romanesque style. Nearby, the Chapelle du Nord (1878) and the Chapelle de la Scala Santa (1891) can also be visited, as can the outdoor stations of the cross.

Mont-Sainte-Anne Park is superb. Its ski-slopes have an excellent reputation, and one can also take part in all kinds of sporting and leisure activities in the park. In the autumn, the different colours of the leaves on the trees offer a sight unequalled by any firework display.

Saint-Ferréol-les-Neiges is a pretty village, though rather sprawling. Four miles to the east of Sainte-Anne-de-Beaupré one comes to the particularly fine Sainte-Anne Falls, which can be admired from above by passing over them on a footbridge.

Twice a year at Cape Tourmente, in spring and autumn, one of the most eagerly-awaited natural phenomena in Quebec takes place, the arrival of the geese! They always stop at this spot on their migratory flight. There are about 200,000 of them and they spend several weeks here, the time necessary to build up the reserves of fat which they need to set off either for the Arctic or for the south of the Unites States, according to the season.

Above: view over the Côte de Beaupré.
Opposite: the famous sanctuary of Ste-Anne-de-Beaupré.

THE ISLAND OF ORLÉANS

It would be inconceivable for anyone wanting to know all about Québec to miss out the island of Orléans. Situated less than seven miles from the centre of the capital, this island, classified as a "historic site" stands as a symbol of the beginnings of the colonization of New France. As one travels round the island (a distance of 42 miles) one cannot help but admire the Norman-style houses, the stone churches, the tiny, impressive processionary chapels and the windmills.

Jacques Cartier called it the Island of Bacchus, because of the vines which were to be found there in great numbers, but the name was changed to honour the Duke of Orléans. The first European settlers arrived there only in 1648. In 1759, General Wolfe and his troops came there to prepare the siege of Quebec.

The island today boasts six villages, Sainte-Pétronille, Saint-Laurent, Saint-Jean, Saint-François, Sainte-Famille and Saint-Pierre. It is a favourite haunt for artists and craftsmen, who appreciate its peace and quiet.

A bridge links the island of Orléans to the mainland (level with the Montmorency Falls) but until the bridge was built in 1935, the only way to reach the island was by boat during the summer, and by means of an "ice bridge" during the winter. This was a track marked out on the frozen surface of the river.

Sainte-Pétronille is the most recent of the six parishes. The Hurons, in the 17th century, took refuge at this spot, in order to protect themselves from attacks by the Iroquois. From Sainte-Pétronille there is a splendid view over the town of Quebec and the river.

It was at Saint-Laurent that the boats necessary for the islanders before the construction of the bridge used to be built. Note there the Gosselin Mill (17th century).

Saint-Jean is a very pretty village where pilots and navigators used to live. Picturesque brick houses, built between 1830 and 1880, line the road. They are most attractive with their rather unstable look and their wide range of colours. Also not to be missed: the Mauvide-Genest Manor House (1735) and the 1732 parish church.

After driving through some delightful countryside, one will come to the church of Saint-François (1734), at which a stop must be made. In 1759, it was used as a military hospital for the British troops.

Then the road curves round and one reaches the other side of the island where touristic spots are rather more rare. This part of the island has a much more rural aspect.

Sainte-Famille is the oldest of the parishes. Its church (1749) and a charming processionary chapel are what especially attracts the visitor's attention. It is at Sainte-Famille that is to be found the largest concentration of houses dating from the time of the French regime.

The island of Orléans. A wayside cross, and a villa with a garden. Right: two different views of the rural part of the island.

AROUND QUEBEC CITY

The immediate surroundings of Quebec are, of course, the Beaupré coast, the island of Orléans and the Beauce, but the possibilities for excursions are numerous and interesting to the west and north of the capital.

Following the river westward from Quebec, one skirts a number of delightful villages, and one should not content oneself simply with following the road, but should take the time to pass through the streets of the villages themselves. Neuville, founded in 1679, in the ancient Seigniory of Neuville, was for a long time called Pointe-aux-Trembles. The church, dating from 1696, and the cluster of houses make a halt worthwhile. Donnacona, the following village, is named after a Huron big chief, whom Jacques Cartier took to France in 1535. Cartier had lived through a very difficult winter that year in that very spot, with his men who were suffering from scurvy.

It was to a place not far from Cap-Santé that the survivors of Montcalm's army withdrew after the defeat of the Heights of Abraham, the last place to surrender to the English, five days after the capitulation of Montreal. The church dates from 1755.

After Portneuf, with its many traditional houses, comes Deschambault, one of the most remarkable villages on this road. The superb

Above: the famous "Chemin du Roy", along the St. Lawrence.

82

panorama over the river, the presbytery (1735) and the church (1837), the old houses lining the road and the La Chevrotière mill form a most attractive whole.

The area inland also deserves a leisurely visit. The Duchesnay Forestry Educative Centre invites the visitor to linger a while. The Village-des-Hurons, near Lorretteville, is very well-known in Quebec for its Indian craft products: jewellery, snowshoes, mocassins, clothes made of skins, etc. The chapel, dating from 1731, houses a small museum. The streets all bear the names of Indian chiefs.

The plan of the town of Charlesbourg (formerly a Royal Borough) was based on the "right-angle" idea, with the land allotted to the farmers radiating out from around the church. This method of construction made it easier to set up defences against attacks by Indians.

Further north stand Tewkesbury and Stoneham, lost deep in the heart of the country, situated near the river Jacques Cartier, of which the valley, near the entrance to the Laurentide Park, abounds in possibilities for sporting activitives.

Lake Delage and Lake Beauport are attractive skiing resorts, which means that it is possible for those who live in the capital to ski within less than half-an-hour's drive from home.

Left: the former presbytery of Batiscan and a historic presbyterian house at Deschambault, dating from 1735. Right: a little chapel on the Chemin du Roy.

THE LOWER ST. LAWRENCE

Situated on the way to la Gaspésie, the Lower St. Lawrence area deserves to be explored to the full. Unfortunately, there are too many visitors who rush through the area without stopping to do this. Vikings came here several hundreds of years ago, then Basque fishermen, but the town really started to develop after 1860 when the railway reached the region. Nowadays, the inhabitants live by fishing, agriculture and lumbering.

After La Pocatière, where the regional museum is attractively original, the road runs between the St. Lawrence and the Appalachian Mountains, surrounded by pastureland. The visitor should make the effort to go out of his way as far as the Rivière-Ouelle quay.

Kamouraska ("where there are rushes beside the water" in Indian language) is a delightful village, very well known throughout Quebec. The houses are huddled close beside each other. Langlais House (1750) has a great deal of charm. Facing the village, the archipelago of Kamouraska is formed by the Grosse-Ile and the islands called les Harengs, les Cornailles, les Patins, Brulées and la Providence.

Soon after this point, a road running inland allows one to reach the little region of the Témiscouata. Those who like walking will enjoy the Parke reserve. It is said that a monster lies hidden in the waters of Lake Pohénégamook.

Another road, still in the Témiscouata, passes through Cabano and Notre-Dame-du-Lac, a historical route called the Grand-Portage road. It is a kind of natural corridor used by the Indians and the early settlers to go from 'Acadia to Quebec'. At Cabano, near the magnificent Lake Témiscouata, Ingall Fort (1839), built in wood, is unique of its kind.

Returning to the road along the St. Lawrence, one will pass through Notre-Dame-du-Portage. Legend has it that the Devil lived there in a rock (Malin Rock) and ran after the villagers in the shape of a veiled giant or of a dog.

On the coast between Rivière-Ouelle and Trois-Pistoles, wooden poles can be seen sticking out of the water. They are called "fascines" and they are used as traps for catching eels. The posts are joined together with branches of spruce and cherry-wood and they force the eels to swim towards the traps which the fishermen bring to catch them in when they come in flat boats at low tide.

Rivière-du-Loup is a pleasant little town. The origin of its name is not known. Does it come from the name of a French ship, *Le Loup,* or from an Indian tribe, the Mahigans, whose name means

Above: pastureland beside the St. Lawrence. Left: a signboard, a reminder of History... a patrician house in Loretteville. Opposite, left and right: two views of the pretty little village of Rivière-du-Loup. Right, top: a steamer... a Russian steamer, on the majestic waters of the St. Lawrence.

"loups' (wolves), or again perhaps from the presence in earlier days of a number of "sea-wolves" (seals) at this spot? On the little island called "île Verte", lying opposite the village of "L'Isle Verte", stands the oldest lighthouse in the province of Quebec (1809).

In 1621, a boatman who had dropped a goblet into the river, is said to have cried out, "That is three pistoles lost?" Trois-Pistoles owes its name to this incident. On the island of les Basques, olds ovens used to extract oil from whales recall the time when Basque fishermen lived here.

There are a number of little islands lying off Bic, a village set amongst mountains. Legend relates that the angel entrusted with the task of arranging the relief of the earth arrived at Bic at the end of the day with a surplus of mountains and islands, and got rid of them here! The country is really superb.

At Rimouski, a large industrial and commercial centre, and a university town of the Lower St. Lawrence, the cathedral, dating from 1862 and the regional museum, housed in the oldest church in the town, are both worth the visitor's attention.

On 29th May 1914, one of the worst shipwrecks in history took place off Sainte-Luce, when the luxurious English liner *Empress of Ireland* went down with the loss of 1,014 lives.

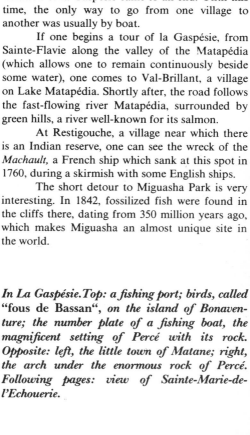

LA GASPESIE

The peninsula of la Gaspésie is without any doubt the part of Quebec that is most popular with tourists. It deserves its reputation, since it can offer the sea, mountains and forests everywhere, as well as being incredibly beautiful.

In 1534, Jacques Cartier explored what was to be the bay of les Chaleurs, and landed on 16th July on the present site of Gaspé, where he had a large cross set up, thus taking possession of this land in the name of the king of France. Three hundred Amerindians were present. In 1603, Champlain gave the place the name of "Gachapé", from the Indian word "Gespeg" which means "end of the land" in the language of the Micmacs.

La Gaspésie was populated during the 18th century by the arrival of members of different communities: Acadians, English loyalists, Scotsmen, Irishmen... It was not until 1929, when the road round the peninsula was finished, that the isolation of la Gaspésie came to an end. Until this time, the only way to go from one village to another was usually by boat.

If one begins a tour of la Gaspésie, from Sainte-Flavie along the valley of the Matapédia (which allows one to remain continuously beside some water), one comes to Val-Brillant, a village on Lake Matapédia. Shortly after, the road follows the fast-flowing river Matapédia, surrounded by green hills, a river well-known for its salmon.

At Restigouche, a village near which there is an Indian reserve, one can see the wreck of the *Machault,* a French ship which sank at this spot in 1760, during a skirmish with some English ships.

The short detour to Miguasha Park is very interesting. In 1842, fossilized fish were found in the cliffs there, dating from 350 million years ago, which makes Miguasha an almost unique site in the world.

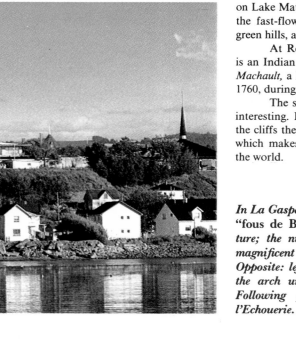

In La Gaspésie. Top: a fishing port; birds, called "fous de Bassan", on the island of Bonaventure; the number plate of a fishing boat, the magnificent setting of Percé with its rock. Opposite: left, the little town of Matane; right, the arch under the enormous rock of Percé. Following pages: view of Sainte-Marie-de-l'Echouerie.

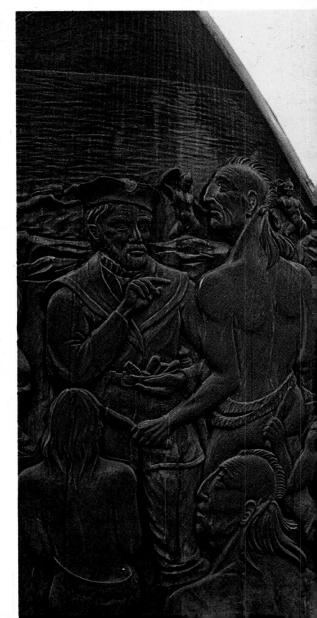

The ascension to the summit of Mount Saint-Joseph (1,980 feet) gives the climber the opportunity to admire almost the whole of the bay of les Chaleurs. In the Indian reserve of Maria, where the Micmacs live, the church is built in the shape of a tepee.

And then there is Percé! One cannot help but admire this grandiose site, and it is not surprising that Percé is one of the most touristic towns in Quebec. The rock of the same name, which stands facing the town, is a huge block of chalk rising from the water and pierced *(percé* in French) at the end. Also off Percé is the amazing island of Bonaventure, on which from April to November live 50,000 *"fous de Bassan"* — white birds with black wing-tips and a saffron-yellow head. Only twenty-two colonies of *fous de Bassan*

Above: facing the famous Percé (Pierced) Rock, a beautiful house, curiously perched aloft. Left: a residence in the traditional style of North America, in the Valley of the Matapédia. Right, top: one of the magnificent waterfalls of La Gaspésie. Below: detail of a monument in memory of Jacques Cartier, at Gaspé.

are known of in the world. Nesting on the ledges of this wild-looking island, these birds create an extraordinary atmosphere there.

At Gaspé, the largest town in la Gaspésie, a visit should be made to the Regional Museum of History and Popular Traditions, as well as the cathedral, built of cedar-wood. Forillon Park provides a number of surprises. At one end of it, at Cap-Bon-Ami, thousands of birds (160 different species) hide their nests in the cliffs.

The north coast of La Gaspésie is particularly remarkable. The road goes up and down, running first along the top of high sheer cliffs, then at river level, only a few feet from the water. The villages along the road have poetic names, such as: L'Anse-au-Griffon, Rivière-au-Renard (the most important centre for fishing in Quebec), Anse-Pleureuse, Ruisseau-Castor...

The two villages of Mont-Louis and Mont-Saint-Pierre are situated in such a position that not one of their buildings can hide the view of the river. The attractive lighthouse of La Martre stands perched on a high point on the top of a hill. Two natural monoliths rise from the long stretch of beach at Saint-Joachim-de-Tourelle. Sainte-Anne-des-Monts is an agricultural and forestry centre, from which one can take a road that leads to the heart of the Chic-Choc mountains. It is possible to climb to the top of Mount Albert (3,870 feet) and Mount Jacques Cartier (4,225 feet). The countryside is grandiose, the type of vegetation arctic: creeping shrubs, mosses, lichen... With a bit of luck, one can catch a glimpse of caribous.

Back on the coast, a stop must be made at Matane, to see the salmon in the migratory passage as they make their way up the river. Between Métis-sur-Mer and Grand-Métis, the Métis gardens contain 2,500 different species of flowers and plants.

THE ISLANDS OF LA MADELEINE

Nobody can remain indifferent to the islands of La Madeleine. In fact, most people fall in love with them. The traveller who has time to land on these islands, lost in the Gulf of the St. Lawrence, will not forget the marvellous trip nor regret making the detour.

How could one, indeed, remain unmoved at the sight of those golden beaches—there are nearly 200 miles of them—virtually deserted, the little fishing harbours, the dunes of a delicate shade of green, the houses of different colours, dotted about here and there, the "hay-stores" made up of just four posts and a little roof?

How could one remain insensitive to the welcome of the Madelinots, whose enjoyment of every celebration gives an added boost to a stay in the islands? The Acadians, who make up the majority of the population, speak a coulourful language, full of nautical terms.

In 1534, Jacques Cartier gave these islands the name of "Les Araynes" and Champlain called them the "Iles Ramées"; they owe their present name to the first Lord of the Islands, who was called Madeleine at the end of the 17th century.

It was on the Islands of La Madeleine in 1597 that the first battle on the American continent between the British and the French took place, a battle won by the French.

The real settlement of the islands began in 1755 when the Acadians, deported from Nova Scotia, at the time of the "Great Botheration Scheme" took refuge here.

In the 19th century the Madelinots were victims of the intolerance of the English lords, who had been given this region, and a large number of them decided to return home during this period. In 1895, a Quebec law gave them the opportunity of buying their land. From that time on, the islands have steadily developed and the islanders (numbering some 15,000, several hundred of them of Scottish descent) earn their living mainly through fishing and tourism.

Every spring, when the drift-ice of the gulf breaks up, a large number of fishermen set off in search of sea-perch or seals. This represents for the population of the islands more than a very old tradition, it is a real source of revenue, and if this activity is criticized in many countries, here the inhabitants produce special justification for it.

The archipelago is composed of seven main islands, six of which are linked to each other by bridges, as well as a number of small uninhabited islands.

Further out to sea is the island of 'Entrée, which can only be reached by boat, then Grande Entrée, a centre for lobster-catching. On the island of Havre-Aubert, where Bassin and Havre-Aubert are two sea-ports, one must visit the Museum of the Sea, which retraces especially the history of the numerous shipwrecks that have taken place in the area. Cap-aux-Meules, on the island of the same name, acts as a kind of capital for the archipelago. It is a busy port, with cargo-ships and ferry-boats constantly arriving or leaving.

Left: the red rocks on a beach of the Islands of La Madeleine and the little harbour on one of the islands. Each spring, seals come onto the islands; their babies are born here (above). While the children play hockey, fishermen and huntsmen often have to carry their boats across the ice. Opposite: pastureland on the islands in summer.

NEW QUEBEC

Going to New Quebec is a real adventure! This vast territory (it represents 51% of the area covered by Quebec) is almost completely deserted, since, apart from those working on sites there, only a few thousand Inuits, or Eskimoes, and Cris Indians live there.

It was while searching for the India route aboard the *Discovery* that Henri Hudson discovered, in 1610, the bay that was to bear his name. As for Thomas James it was aboard the wonderful *Henrietta Maria* that he sailed into the future James Bay.

The Hudson's Bay Company, set up in 1670, had as its aim the organization of the fur trade in New France.

However, its first trading-post in eskimo territory was only established in 1830 (at Kujjuaq, now called Fort Chimo).

The James Bay project first saw the light of day in 1971. Gigantic sites sprang up then, the work being mainly concentrated on the Great River, 500 miles long, the largest stretch of water in the region.

Altogether, the laying out of the four sites of the Complex, LG1, LG2, LG3 and LG4, as well as six reservoirs, necessitated the erection of nine dams, 170 dykes and nine power-stations.

The 5,000 Inuits of Quebec all live in New Quebec, in about fifteen coastal villages situated on the northern perimeter of the province. Their hospitality is legendary.

Left: a lake in the Chibougamau Park in New Quebec, polar bears on the ice, a polar-bear skin which has just been cut and a beaver-"hut" in a nature park. Above: Eskimos with their teams of dogs and their fishing-canoes; their traditional costumes must be admired. Below: dykes on James Bay.

Last page: the amazing Montmorency falls, one of the beauties, one of the many beauties, which nature has to offer in Quebec.

Most of them are engaged in temporary work, but some of them take up sculpture, using walrus tusks, caribou horns and steatite, a silicate of natural magnesium, to work on. Their works generally represent scenes of daily life: hunting, fishing, family life in an igloo, etc.

In this extraordinary territory, the fauna is very special: caribous are found there, and polar bears, black bears, whales, walruses and narwhals. A few musk oxen are also raised there, though it was necessary first of all to go and fetch the first of them from Greenland.

They are released into their natural surroundings after the "quiviut", a natural light, warm fibres, has been removed from them.

It is in the Torngat massif that the highest summits of the eastern part of North America are to be found, with Mount Iberville reaching a height of some 5,850 feet.

The New Quebec Crater, discovered in 1945, has a diameter of 12,500 feet and encloses a lake 900 feet deep, of which the water is frozen the whole year, except during a short period of 45 days in the summer.

As for the midnight sun, it can be seen from here and it is an incomparable sight!